Treasured Stories

By

LUCY GERTSCH THOMSON

BOOKCRAFT

Salt Lake City

TREASURED STORIES

A book of faith-promoting stories
and unforgetable sermons

by

Lucy Gertsch Thomson

Author and compiler of:

Little Stepping Stones
Stories that Live
Somewhere I've Read
Women of the Bible
Minute Masterpieces

Lovingly

Dedicated to the Frodsham

Triplets — Mary, Ruth and Eve.

Preface

This compilation of faith-promoting stories and stimulating sermons was prepared with the sincere hope that the faith of all those who read these true experiences might be increased.

Elder Ballard of the Council of the Twelve was once asked if he thought he could ever lose his testimony. He replied, "I'd hate to be away from the Church for more than six months."

One's spirituality soon deteriorates through inactivity, plus the absence of religious reading. My earnest desire is to place good literature among our rising generation, so it may help to instil faith and integrity in the minds of our youth.

May youth ever remember that this life is the time to prepare for God; that their judgment will be based upon their deeds, done in the flesh. Our life is our record and shall stand forever as the following poem of Zelda Howard suggests:

LIFE IS A BOOK

Life is a book made up of days;
 Each one of us writes one;
It's opened when we come to earth
 And closed when life is done.

No pen but ours ere touches it,
 In our own way we write,
Whether we fail or we succeed,
 Turns with the page at night.

And there is no erasing it
 To add or take away,
The yesterday's account is closed,
 Sealed within white or gray.

The morning gives another sheet
 That's broad and very white,
And oh, how glorious to have
 Another chance to write!

No bad is there too small to show,
 No good that's ever lost,
All that we do goes into Life's book
 In black and white embossed.

—*Zelda Davis Howard*

Acknowledgments

Deep appreciation is given to Elaine Lunn and Marion Mortenson for typing the manuscript.

Also sincere thanks is extended to those who gave permission to use the following:

To Zelda Davis Howard for her poem, "Life is a Book."

To the George Albert Smith family for: "Your Good Name," and "A Story of Two Boys."

To Mrs. Don McBride for permission to use: "God Moves in a Mysterious Way"; and "The Retreat."

To Archibald Bennett, of the Genealogical Society, for: "Records Divinely Given," "Stopped by a Voice," and "A Change of Plans."

To Elder Hugh B. Brown for: "A Lieutenants' Courage."

To Lucy G. Cannon for: "In the Hour of Parting."

To Clara Middlemiss for: "A Terrifying Experience."

7

To Brother Samuel Blue for permission to use: "Samuel Blue's Triumph."

To Elder Spencer Kimball for permission to use: "Be Ye Clean, A Style of our Own," and "Except Ye Repent."

To Elder Harold B. Lee and Pres. Ernest L. Wilkinson for permission to use: "Unfinished Business."

To the Deseret News Press for permission to use: "You May Come Back."

To the Deseret Book Co. for: "Rather be a Deacon," and 'Saved from Death.'

To the Instructor magazine for permission to use: "A Remarkable Conversion, Evil Spirits, Healings at Commerce, Saved from a Mob," and 'You Will Get Those Arms.'

Table of Contents

Table of Contents
(continued)

A Remarkable Conversion

(Excerpts copied from "Early Scenes In Church History," eighth book of the Faith-Promoting Series. JUVENILE INSTRUCTOR OFFICE, Salt Lake City, 1882. From chapter SCENES IN THE BRITISH MISSION . . . Brother Halliday . . . relates (an) instance in which the power of God was displayed in a rather remarkable manner, . . .)

He and Elder John Chislett were sent to Penzance, Cornwall, to introduce the gospel to the inhabitants. They met with no encouragement, yet they did not feel justified in leaving the place until they had given the people a thorough warning. Their funds were so low that the two of them were forced to live on a penny's worth of bread and a penny's worth of soup per day; yet their faith was strong, and they spent much of their time in prayer. Finally as a last resort, in the effort to awaken an interest in the message they had to bear to the people, they decided to give a course of public lectures. Elder Halliday pawned his watch to raise the necessary money to rent a hall and publish some placards announcing their meetings, and on the first evening appointed they were gratified at seeing a few come to hear them. Among the audience they noticed particularly a well-dressed gentleman and lady, the latter of whom commenced weeping almost as soon as she entered the hall and continued to do so as long as the meeting lasted. The elders, of course, could assign no reason for this peculiar conduct while the meeting was in progress, nor were they any more enlightened when, at the close of the services, the lady came forward with her husband and invited them to visit at her home at St. Just, about six miles distant. This was the first invitation they had received from anyone in the place, and they accepted it joyfully and would willingly have gone home with her that night, but, to their disappointment, she named the following Wednesday as the time when she would be pleased to receive them. The elders continued to subsist upon their scanty fare, and spent their time in vainly endeavoring to proselyte among the citizens of Penzance.

Wednesday morning came and with it a drenching rainstorm, through which the elders tramped the whole six miles, hungry and penniless. Shortly before arriving at St. Just, and while they were crossing a plowed field, with the mud clinging to their boots so they could scarcely walk, the Lord deigned to comfort them by giving Elder Halliday the gift of tongues and the interpretation of the same, in which it was made known to him that the lady whom they were going to visit had been favored with a vision in which she had seen himself and Elder Chislett; also that she was the owner of several houses, one of which she was going to allow them to use to hold meetings in, and that he was going to baptize her that very night.

As soon as this had passed through his mind, for he had not spoken aloud, but to himself, he joyfully slapped his companion on the shoulder and exclaimed, "Cheer up, John! I have had a revelation!" He then proceeded to relate all that had been revealed to him.

When they arrived at the house, they were drenched as badly as if they had been in a river. Even their boots were full of water, so that when they pulled them off and turned the tops downward it ran out of them in a stream. Their friend, however, had been anxiously looking for them, and had prepared a blazing fire to warm them and spread the table with tempting food. She also proposed for them to change their clothes as far as she could supply them with dry ones to put on from her husband's wardrobe. "But," said she, "I can hardly wait for you to change your clothes, I am so anxious to talk to you."

"Oh, you need not be in such a hurry," remarked Elder Halliday, "For I know what you are going to say!"

She looked at him in surprise and inquired how he knew.

"Why," he said, "I have had it revealed to me on the way here." He then related to her every particular as it had been made known to him, until he got to that part relating to her baptism, when she interrupted him by exclaiming in surprise to her husband:

"There, now, is that not just as it occurred? How could he have learned that? For you know I have not talked with anyone but you about it!" She then admitted that the week previous, while lying awake in bed, she saw a bright light in the room and awoke her husband and pointed it out to him. He also saw it, and it passed around the room in the direction of Penzance, to which place it led her in her mind, and there she saw two men trying to raise a standard, in which labor the people who looked on seemed unwilling to lend a helping hand. She reproached them for their lack of interest and took hold herself to assist. This vision was so plain that she afterwards related the whole of it to her husband and even described the appearance of the men. Then she could not rest until she had, in company with her husband, visited Penzance and attended the lecture she there saw announced. As soon as she entered the hall and saw the two elders she recognized them and could not refrain from crying. As to the other part of what had been revealed to him, she said it was true that she was the owner of a row of houses, which she pointed out to the elders, and that the last one was a schoolhouse in which her husband taught school, and which they were welcome to use as a meetinghouse as long as they wanted to free of charge.

"But," said Elder Halliday, "that is not all that the Lord revealed to me. He told me that I was going to baptize you before I went to bed tonight, and now I want your husband to go and find some water for that purpose."

Brother Halliday, in telling what had been revealed to him, felt a good deal as he imagined the Prophet Jonah must have felt when the Lord commanded him to go to Ninevah and declare the destruction of that city. He had before him the fear of being declared a false prophet, and it required a great deal of faith in him to tell it, especially that part relating to her baptism. However, he was soon relieved on that score, for the good woman expressed her readiness and anxiety to go immediately and be baptized. But her husband declared there was not a stream or pond in that region deep enough to baptize a person in, and it would be no use for them to think of doing such a thing that day. "Is there not a ditch or hollow anywhere around here that is deep enough?" said Elder Halliday, "Please go and see."

The husband complied with a dubious look on his face, while the elders proceeded to change and dry their clothes, and soon he returned and reported that the heavy shower which had fallen had so filled all the ditches and low places that they would have no difficulty in finding water deep enough.

Within two hours from the arrival of the elders the woman was baptized and confirmed, she being the first one to embrace the gospel in the region known as "Land's End."

Compelled to Preach

(Taken from *Leaves From My Journal*, page 16)

On the 27th of March, I arrived at Memphis, weary and hungry. I went to the best tavern in the place, kept by Mr. Josiah Jackson. I told him I was a stranger and had no money. I asked him if he would keep me overnight.

He asked me what my business was.

I told him I was a preacher of the gospel.

He laughed and said that I did not look much like a preacher.

I did not blame him as all the preachers he had ever been acquainted with rode on fine horses or in fine carriages, clothed in broadcloth, and had large salaries, and would see this whole world sink to perdition before they would wade through one hundred and seventy miles of mud to save the people.

The landlord wanted a little fun so he said he would keep me if I would preach. He wanted to see if I could preach.

I must confess that by this time I became a little mischievous, and pleaded with him not to set me preaching.

The more I pleaded to be excused, the more determined Mr. Jackson was that I should preach. He took my valise, and the landlady got me a good supper.

I sat down in a large hall to eat supper. Before I got through, the room began to fill with some of the rich and fashionable of Memphis, dressed in their broadcloth and silk, while my appearance was such as you can imagine, after traveling through the mud as I had been.

When I had finished eating, the table was carried out of the room over the heads of the people. I was placed in the corner of the room with a stand having a Bible, hymnbook and candle on it, hemmed in by a dozen men with the landlord in the center.

There weer present some *five hundred persons* who had come together, not to hear a gospel sermon but to have some fun.

Now, boys, how would you like this position? On your first mission, without a companion or friend, and to be called upon to preach to such a congregation? With me it was one of the most pleasing hours of my life, although I felt as though I should like company.

I read a hymn and asked them to sing. Not a soul would sing a word.

I told them I had not the gift of singing; but with the help of the Lord, I would both pray and preach. I knelt down to pray and the men around me dropped on their knees. I prayed to the Lord to give me his Spirit and to show me the hearts of the people. I promised the Lord in my prayer I would deliver to that congregation whatever he would give to me. I arose and spoke one hour and a half, and it was one of the best sermons of my life.

The lives of the congregation were opened to the vision of my mind and I told them of their wicked deeds and the reward they would obtain. The men who surrounded me dropped their heads. Three minutes after I closed I was the only person in the room.

Soon I was shown to a bed in a room adjoining a large one in which were assembled many of the men whom I had been preaching to. I could hear their conversation.

One man said he would like to know how that Mormon boy knew of their past lives.

In a little while they got to disputing about some doctrinal point. One suggested calling me to decide the point. The landlord said, "No, we have had enough for once."

In the morning, I had a good breakfast. The landlord said if I came that way again to stop at his house and stay as long as I might choose.

Raised from Death

(Taken from *Leaves From My Journal*, page 53)

On the 23rd of November my wife, Phoebe, was attacked with a severe headache, which terminated in brain fever. She grew more and more distressed daily as we continued our journey. It was a terrible ordeal for a woman to travel in a wagon over rough roads, afflicted as she was. At the same time our child was also very sick.

The first of December was a trying day to my soul. My wife continued to fail and in the afternoon about four o'clock, she appeared to be struck with death. I stopped my team, and it seemed as if she would breathe her last lying in the wagon. Two of the sisters sat beside her to see whether they could do anything for her in her last moments.

I stood upon the ground in deep affliction and meditated. I cried unto the Lord and prayed that she might live and not be taken from me. I claimed the promises the Lord had made unto me through the prophets and patriarchs, and soon her spirit revived. I drove a short distance to a tavern and got her into a room and worked over her and her babe all night, and prayed to the Lord to preserve her life.

In the morning the circumstances were such that I was under the necessity of removing my wife from the inn because there was so much noise and confusion at the place that she could not endure it. I carried her out to her bed in the wagon and drove two miles. I alighted at a house and carried my wife and her bed into it, with determination to tarry there until she either recovered her health or passed away. This was on Sunday morning.

After getting my wife and things into the house and wood provided to keep up a fire, I employed my time in taking care of her. It looked as if she had but a short time to live.

She called me to her bedside in the evening and said she felt as if a few moments more would end her existence in this life. She manifested great confidence in the cause she had embraced and exhorted me to have confidence in God and to keep his commandments.

To all appearances she was dying. I laid hands upon her and prayed for her and she soon revived and slept a little during the night.

December 3rd found my wife very low. I spent the day in taking care of her, and the following day I returned to Eaton to get some things for her. She seemed to be gradually sinking and in the evening her spirit apparently left her body, and she was dead.

The sisters gathered around her body and wept, while I stood looking at her in sorrow. The spirit and power of God began to rest upon me and for the first time during her sickness, faith filled my soul, although she lay before me as one dead.

I had some oil that had been consecrated for my anointing while in Kirtland. I took it and consecrated it again before the Lord for anointing the sick. I then bowed down before the Lord and prayed for the life of my companion, and I anointed her body with the oil in the name of the Lord. I laid my hands upon her, and in the name of Jesus Christ I rebuked the power of death and the destroyer, and commanded the same to depart from her, and the spirit of life to enter her body.

Her spirit returned to her body and from that hour she was made whole. We all felt to praise the name of God and to trust in him and to keep his commandments.

While this operation was going on with me (as my wife related afterwards) her spirit left her body, and she saw her body lying upon the bed, and the sisters weeping. She looked at them and at me, and upon her babe, and while gazing upon this scene, two personages came into the room carrying a coffin, and told her they had come for her body. One of these messengers informed her that she could have her choice; she might go to rest in the spirit world, or on one condition she could have the privilege of returning to her tabernacle and continuing her labors upon the earth. The condition was, if she felt that she could stand by her husband, and with him pass through all the cares, trials, tribulations, and afflictions of life which he would be called to pass through for the gospel's sake unto the end. When she looked at the situation of her husband and child she said: "Yes, I will do it!"

At the moment that decision was made the power of faith rested upon me, and when I administered unto her, her spirit entered her tabernacle, and she saw the messengers carry the coffin out at the door.

A Change of Plans

(Related by Mark Austin, former
president of the Fremont Stake)

In the spring of 1897, I was laboring in the British Mission. Elder J. W. West came as a missionary and was appointed to labor with me. His father had gone from London to Utah about forty years prior to that time, having been previously engaged in the book-binding business. He had told his son just before the latter left for the mission, that there were a number of good young men with whom he had worked in London, who had since died, and he was strongly impressed with the thought that he ought to do the work for them in the temple. He gave his son a list of the names and told him that his younger brother, living in London, a jeweler by trade, would help to locate, if possible, a man by the name of Proburt, who was also one of his friends, and who he felt sure was yet alive. Mr. Proburt would no doubt help him to get the information concerning their friends.

Elder West and I went to London to inquire concerning Mr. Proburt but were unsuccessful so we decided to give up. I concluded to go to Dunstable, thirty miles north and visit my mother's only sister, while Elder West would visit his uncle. When he had visited with his uncle, he was to come my way, and together we would return to our field of labor. The next morning, however, Elder West decided to accompany me and return another time to visit his relatives.

I was delighted to have him join me. We visited my aunt and then one of my uncles. When we returned to the home of my aunt, we discovered she had gone for a ride with a friend and his wife.

In a short time she returned and said to Elder West, "Where did your people go from when they went to Utah?"

"From London," said Elder West.

"Did your father know a man by the name of Proburt?"

"Yes," he answered.

"Well, I have been out riding with Mr. Proburt and his wife, the first time since they have lived here, about twenty years. I was telling them that I had a nephew, and his friend West visiting me from Utah. He was impressed with the thought that you might be the son of his old friend who had gone from London many years before. He has gone home to unhitch the horse and will be back."

In a few minutes Mr. Proburt came in, and as soon as he saw Elder West, he said, "I think you are the son of my friend."

After further conversation in regard to his father and family, Mr. Proburt said, "A few months ago I said to my wife, I am strongly impressed with the thought that I ought to go up to London and get the gene-alogy of a number of my old friends who worked with me in the bookbinding business — good young men, who have since died. I did so and have made the record, and I was wondering, Mr. West, whether your father would have any use for it?"

Elder West answered, "Yes, my father would be delighted to get that information. He asked me to try and find you and said you would help me."

Mr. Proburt immediately went home and secured the records and information.

The unbeliever may say this was purely accidental, but I say to all I was impressed and so was Elder West when he changed his plans.

A Patriarchal Blessing

(Taken from *Leaves From My Journal*, by Wilford Woodruff, page 93-96)

Father Joseph Smith, the father of the Prophet Joseph Smith, was the first Patriarch to the Church of Jesus Christ of Latter-day Saints. He gave a great many blessings unto the Saints, which are recorded, and many of them have seen their fulfilment.

When he put his hands on the head of a person to bless him, it seemed as if the heavens were opened, and he could reveal the whole life of that person.

He gave me my patriarchal blessing in the temple of the Lord at Kirtland, on the 15th day of April, 1837.

Many marvelous things which he sealed upon my head, for which I could then see no earthly chance of fulfilment, have already been fulfilled to the very letter.

One or two instances I will name. He said I should have access to the treasures hid in the ground to assist me in getting myself and others to Zion.

When in Cambridgeport gathering up the Saints in 1850, Alexander Badlam went to California on business and the Saints who were digging gold filled a little sack with gold dust and sent it to me to assist me on my mission.

By the sale of this treasure from California I was enabled to emigrate with my family and a number of others to Zion in the mountains.

He also said I should have power to bring my father and his family into the Church. This was fulfilled when I visited them during my mission to the Fox Islands.

My father gathered to Salt Lake City with the Saints and he died there, aged 83 years.

The Patriarch also said I should be wrapt in the visions of heaven and an angel of God should teach me many things. This was literally fulfilled.

Again, he told me I should be delivered from my enemies (who would seek my destruction) by the mighty power of God and the administrations of angels. This was marvelously fulfilled while in the city of London in 1840. Brothers Heber C. Kimball, George A. Smith, and I went to London together in the winter of 1840, being the first elders who had attempted to establish the gospel in that great and mighty city.

As soon as we commenced we found the devil was manifest: The evil spirits gathered for our destruction, and at times they had great power.

They would destroy all the Saints if they were not restrained by the power of God.

Brother Smith and I were together and had retired to our rest, each occupying a cot but three feet apart.

We had only just lain down when it seemed as if a legion of devils made war upon us. They tried to destroy us and we were struggling for our lives in the midst of this warfare of evil spirits until we were nearly choked to death.

I began to pray the best that I could in the midst of this struggle and asked the Father in the name of Jesus Christ to spare our lives.

While thus praying three personages entered the room, clothed in white and encircled with light.

They walked to our bedside, laid hands upon our heads, and we were instantly delivered: From that time forth we were no more troubled with evil spirits while in the city of London.

As soon as the personages administered unto us they withdrew from the room; the lights withdrew with them; and darkness returned.

Many other sayings of the Patriarch Joseph Smith in my blessing have been fulfilled in my experience but I have said sufficient upon this subject. All the blessings that are sealed upon our heads will be fulfilled, and many more, if we are faithful and live for them.

In closing my testimony I wish to say that I do not think that the Lord ever sends an angel to the earth to visit the children of men unless it is necessary to introduce a dispensation of the gospel, or deliver a message, or perform a work that cannot be done otherwise.

It required an angel of God to deliver the gospel to Joseph Smith because it was not then upon the earth, and that was in fulfilment of the word of the Lord through John the Revelator. (Revelation XIV 6.) And so in regard to the administration of angels in all ages of the world, it is to deliver a message and perform a work which cannot otherwise be accomplished.

A Terrifying Experience

The question is often asked, "Do we really have revelation today?" A very impressive incident happened in Hawaii, in answer to this question.

It happened in 1921 while President McKay and Elder Hugh Cannon were making a tour of the missions of the world. After a day of inspiring conference meetings in Hilo, Hawaii, a night trip to the Kilauea volcano was arranged for the visiting brethren and some of the missionaries. About nine o'clock that evening, two carloads of us, took off for the then very active volcano.

We stood on the rim of that fiery pit watching Pele in her satanic antics, our backs chilled by the cold winds sweeping down from the snow-capped Mauna Loa, and our faces almost blistered by the heat of the molten lava. Tiring of the cold, one of the elders discovered a volcanic balcony about four feet down inside the crater where observers could watch the display without being chilled by the wind. It seemed perfectly sound, and the "railing" on the open side of it formed a fine

protection from the intense heat, making it
an excellent place to view the spectacular display.

After first testing its safety, Brother Mc-
Kay and three of the elders climbed down
into the hanging balcony. As they stood there
warm and comfortable, they teased the others
of us more timid ones who had hesitated to
take advantage of the protection they had
found. For quite some time we all watched
the ever-changing sight as we alternately
chilled and roasted.

After being down there in their protected
spot for some time, suddenly Brother McKay
said to those with him, "Brethren, I feel impressed that we should get out of here."

With that he assisted the elders to climb
out, and then they in turn helped him up to
the wind-swept rim. It seems incredible, but
almost immediately the whole balcony crum-
bled and fell with a roar into the molten lava
a hundred feet or so below.

It is easy to visualize the feelings of those
who witnessed this terrifying experience. Not
a word was said . . . the whole thing was too

awful, with all that word means. The only sound was the hiss and roar of Pele, the Fire Goddess of old Hawaii, screaming her disappointment.

None of us who were witnesses to this experience could ever doubt the reality of "revelation in our day!" Some might say it was merely inspiration, but to us, it was a direct revelation given to a worthy man.

$\mathscr{D}$

God Moves in a Mysterious Way

V-E day caused happiness and gratitude among the European nations. Freedom and all that it signified had gained a tremendous victory over the power of evil. But now everyone, although elated in spirit, faced the great task of reconstructing cities, roads, and things which had been destroyed.

At the end of the war, President Zimmer had a strong desire to visit war-torn Germany and administer to the spiritual and physical needs of the Saints there. For three decades he had travelled extensively in the German-speaking part of Europe in Church assignments. He made repeated application to the officials of the U. S. Army to enter Germany and Austria, with no success. It seemed impossible for any civilian to enter into occupied Germany. President Zimmer, nevertheless, felt very strongly that he was much needed there. He and his family made it a matter of prayer and fasted for several days. Once again the Lord intervened, and Max Zimmer was granted permission to enter Germany. This was nothing short of a miracle for at that time, in fall of 1945, the U. S. Army had issued only five military permits to civilians.

With this problem solved there remained still the almost insurmountable obstacle of how to get into Germany. There were no train connections from Switzerland into Germany at that time, and no gasoline was available for private cars. But President Zimmer was determined to go on foot, if necessary.

He again brought the matter before the Lord and started to make necessary preparations for leaving. Two days after having been granted permission to visit Germany, he received a telephone call from an L.D.S. serviceman at the border who said he had come in his jeep to pick up President Zimmer and take him into Germany where the Saints had called a conference for the next two days to meet with him.

There was no way in the world that these Saints could have known that President Zimmer had received or even applied for a permit because there was no telephone, telegram, or mail service between Germany and other European countries at that time. This knowledge could only have come as a direct revelation from God.

Inspiration

(Jacob Hamblin's impressions to move camp)

At one time I took my wife three miles up a canyon to gather wild fruit while I hewed timber from the mountain. We had intended to remain overnight but while preparing a place to sleep, a feeling came over me that the Indians were watching with the intention of killing us during the night.

I at once yoked my oxen, put my wife and her babe on the wagon, and went home in the evening. My wife expressed surprise at my movements, and I told her that the Indians were watching us. She wished to know how I knew this and asked if I had seen or heard them. I replied that I knew it on the same principle that I knew that the gospel was true.

The following day I returned to the canyon. Three Indians had come down on the road during the night, and robbed a wagon of a gun, ammunition, and other valuables. One of them, from the size of the track, must have been an Indian known as "Old Big Foot." I thank the Lord that he had warned me in time to save my wife and child as well as myself.

Move Your Carriage

(Taken from *Leaves From My Journal*,
by Wilford Woodruff)

In 1848, after my return to Winter Quarters from our pioneer journey, I was appointed by the Presidency of the Church to take my family and go to Boston to gather up the remnant of the Latter-day Saints and lead them to the valleys of the mountains.

While on my way east I put my carriage into the yard of one of the brethren in Indiana, and Brother Orson Hyde set his wagon by the side of mine, and not more than two feet from it.

Dominicus Carter, of Provo, and my wife and four children were with me. My wife, one child and I went to bed in the carriage, the rest sleeping in the house.

I had been in bed but a short time when a voice said to me:

"Get up, and move your carriage."

It was not thunder, lightning or an earthquake, but the still, smal voice of the Spirit of God — the Holy Ghost.

I told my wife I must get up and move my carriage. She asked: "What for?"

I told her I did not know, only the Spirit told me to do it.

I got up and moved my carriage several rods, and set it by the side of the house.

As I was returning to bed the same Spirit said to me, "Go and move your mules away from that oak tree," which was about one hundred yards north of our carriage.

I moved them to a young hickory grove and tied them up. I then went to bed.

In thirty minutes a whirlwind caught the tree to which my mules had been fastened, broke it off near the ground, and carried it one hundred yards, sweeping away two fences in its course, and laid it prostrate through that yard where my carriage stood, and the top limbs hit my carriage as it was.

In the morning I measured the trunk of the tree which fell where my carriage had stood, and I found it to be five feet in diameter. It came within a foot of Brother Hyde's wagon, but did not touch it.

Thus, by obeying the revelation of the Spirit of God to me I saved my life and the lives of my wife and child, as well as my animals.

In the morning I went on my way rejoicing.

Prompted to Take a Different Path

(Taken from *Leaves From My Journal,*
by Wilford Woodruff)

This same spirit of revelation has been manifested to many of my brethren in their labors in the kingdom of God, one of which I will here name.

Elder Chas. C. Rich was going from Sacramento to San Bernardino with a company of the brethren. He had in his possession a large amount of money to make payment on their land purchase. This was known to some road agents in the vicinity, who gathered a company of robbers and went on ahead of Brother Rich and lay in ambush, intending to kill the "Mormons" and rob them of their money.

Before reaching the company of robbers Brother Rich came to a by-path of trail. The Spirit then told him to take that path.

The brethren with him marveled at his course, not knowing that enemies awaited them, but they arrived in safety at San Bernardino with their lives and money, while the robbers wondered why their prey did not come.

Records Divinely Given

On May 17, 1884, the Logan Temple was dedicated. The second day after the dedication President John Taylor said that all members of the Church who were worthy and who desired to go through the temple might do so the next day. My husband, Henry Ballard, being bishop, was very busy writing out recommendations to all who wished to go through the temple when my daughter Ellen came in with a newspaper in her hand and asked for her father. I told her that her father was very busy and to give the paper to me and I would give it to them. She said, "No, a man gave the paper to me and told me to give it to no one but father."

I let the child take the paper to her father, and when he took it and looked at it he was greatly surprised, for he saw that the paper had been printed in Berkshire, England, his birthplace, and was only four days from the press. He was so amazed at such an incident that he called Ellen and asked her where the man was who had given her the paper. She said she was playing on the sidewalk with

other children when two men came down the
street, walking in the middle of the road,
one of the men called to her saying, "Come
here, little girl." She hesitated at first, for
there were other little girls with her. Then
he pointed to her and said, "You." She went,
and he gave her the paper and told her to
give it to her father.

The paper contained about sixty names of
dead acquaintances of my husband, giving
the dates of birth and death. My husband took
the paper to the president of the temple and
asked him what he thought about it. President
Merrill said, "Brother Ballard, that was one of
the three Nephites or some other person who
brought that paper to you, for it could come in
no other way in so short a time. It is for you
to do the work for them."

My husband was baptized for the men;
and, I for the women; and all of the work was
done for them. Again I felt the Lord was
mindful of us and blessed us abundantly.

Elder Melvin J. Ballard, her son, has giv-
en this added explanation:

"We looked in vain for these travelers.
They were not to be seen. No one else saw

them. Then we turned to the paper. The
newspaper, *The Newbury Weekly News,* was
printed in my father's old English home,
Thursday, May 15, 1884, and reached our
hands May 19, 1884, three days after the
publication. We were astonished, for by no
earthly means could it have reached us, so
that our curiosity increased as we examined
it. Then we discovered one page devoted to
the writings of a reporter of the paper, who
had gone on his vacation, and among other
places had visited an old cemetery. The cur-
ious inscriptions led him to write what he
found on the tombstones, including the verses.
He also added the names, dates of birth,
death, etc., filling nearly an entire page.

"When the matter was presented to President Merrill of the Logan Temple, he said,
'You are authorized to do the work for them
because you received it through messengers
of the Lord.'

"There is no doubt but that the dead who
had received the gospel in the spirit world
had put it into the heart of that reporter to
write these things, and thus the way was prepared for my father to obtain the information

he sought. And so with you who are earnest in this work, the way shall be opened and you will be able to gather data far beyond your expectations. I will tell you what will happen. When you have gone as far as you can go the names of your righteous dead who have embraced the gospel in the spirit world will be given you through the instrumentality of your dead kindred. But only the names of those who have received the gospel will be revealed."

Saved from Death

(An experience of President George Albert Smith)

While laboring in the Southern States as a missionary the following happened:

"Late one evening in a pitch-dark night, Elder Stout and I were traveling along a high precipice. Our little walk was narrow; on one side was the wall of the mountain, on the other side, the deep, deep river. We had no light, and there were no stars and no moon to guide us. We had been traveliig all day, and we knew that we would have hospitality extended to us if we could reach the McKelvin home, which was on the other side of a high valley. We had to cross this mountain in order to reach the home of Mr. McKelvin. Our mode of travel of necessity was very halting. We walked almost with a shuffle, feeling each foot of ground as we advanced, with one hand extended toward the wall of the mountain. Elder Stout was ahead of me, and as I walked along, I felt the hard surface of the trail under my feet. In doing so I left the wall of the mountain which had acted as a guide and a steadying force. After I had taken a few steps away, I felt impressed to stop immediately, that something was wrong. I called to Elder Stout, and he answered me. The direction from which his voice came indicated I was on the wrong trail, so I backed up until I reached the wall of the mountain and again proceeded forward. He was just a few steps in front of me, and as I reached him we came to a fence piling. In the dark we carefully explored it with our hands and feet to see whether it would be safe for us to climb over. We decided that it would be secure and made the effort. While I was on the top of this big pile of logs my little suitcase popped open, and the contents were scattered around. In the dark I felt around for them and was quite convinced I had recovered practically everything. We arrived safely at our destination about eleven o'clock at night. I soon discovered I had lost my comb and brush, and the next morning we returned to the scene of my accident. I recovered my property and while there my curiosity was stimulated and aroused to see what had happened the night before when I had lost my way in the dark. As missionaries, we wore hobnails in the bottom of our shoes to make them last longer, so that I could easily follow our tracks in the soft dirt. I retraced my steps to the point where my tracks left the mountainside and discovered that in the darkness I had wandered to the edge of a deep precipice. Just one more step and I would have fallen into the river and probably been drowned. I felt very ill when I realized how close I had come to death. I also was very grateful to my Heavenly Father for protecting me. I have always felt that if we are doing the Lord's work and ask him for his help and protection, he will guide and take care of us."

Steamboat Disaster

While returning to Utah in 1850 with a large company of Saints from Boston and the east, on my arrival at Pittsburg I engaged a passage for myself and company on a steamer to St. Louis. But no sooner had I engaged the passage than the Spirit said to me, "Go not on board of that steamer, neither you nor your company."

I obeyed the revelation to me, and did not go on board, but took another steamer.

The first seamer started at dark, with 200 passengers on board. When five miles down the Ohio River it took fire, burned the tiller ropes so that the vessel could not reach shore, and the lives of nearly all on board were lost either by fire or water. We arrived in safety at our destination, by obeying the revelation of the Spirit of God to us.

Stopped by a Voice

(An experience of Elder John A. Widtsoe)

"I know of no work that I have done in the Church which has been so filled with testimonies of the divinity of this work as the little I have done in behalf of the salvation of our dead. I could tell you a number of experiences, but the one that impressed me most happened a few years ago when I accompanied Brother Reed Smoot to Europe. He had work to do in Stockholm so I decided to see what I could do in the way of finding books on Swedish genealogy. I knew the names of the two big bookstores in Stockholm. I went to the one, made my selections, and then started across the city to the other bookstore in the hope that I might find some more suitable books. As I hurried along the street filled with people, I was stopped suddenly by some voice which said to me: "Go across the street and down that narrow side street." I looked across the street and saw a little narrow street. I had not been in Stockholm before. I thought: "This is all nonsense, I have little time to spend here. I am not going down that street, I have to do my work. Then the question came,

"What is your business in this city? Are you not on the Lord's errand?" I crossed over; went down the little narrow street, and there, halfway down, found a little bookstore that I had known nothing about. When I asked for books on genealogy, the woman said: "No, we do not carry books on genealogy. When we get such books, we send to the bookstore" — naming the store for which I was headed. Then, just as I was leaving in disappointment, she said: "Stop a minute. A leading book collector, a genealogist, died about a month ago and we bought his library. Many of his genealogical books are in the back room ready to be sent to the bookstore, but if you want to buy them, you may have them." Thus we secured the foundation of Swedish genealogy in our library.

Your Good Name

By President George Albert Smith

A number of years ago I was seriously ill. In fact, I think everyone gave me up but my wife. With my family I went to St. George, Utah, to see if it would improve my health.

eW went as far as we could by train, and then continued the journey in a wagon, in the bottom of which a bed had been made for me.

In St. George we arranged for a tent for my health and comfort, with a built-in floor raised about a foot above the ground, and we could roll up the south side of the tent to make the sunshine and fresh air available. I became so weak as to be scarcely able to move. It was a slow and exhausting effort for me even to turn over in bed.

One day, under these conditions, I lost consciousness of my surroundings and thought I had passed to the other side. I found myself standing with my back to a large and beautiful lake, facing a great forest of trees, There was no one in sight, and there was no boat upon the lake or any other visible means to indicate how I might have arrived there. I realized, or seemed to realize, that I had finished my work in mortality nad had gone home. I began to look around, to see if I could not find someone. There was no evidence of anyone's living there, just those great, beautiful trees in front of me and the wonderful lake behind me.

I began to explore, and soon I found a trail through the woods which seemed to have been used very little, which was almost obscured by grass. I followed this trail, and after I had walked for some time and had traveled a considerable distance through the forest, I saw a man coming towards me. I became aware that he was a very large man and I hurried my steps to reach him because I recognized him as my grandfather. In mortality he weighed over three hundred pounds, so you may know he was a large man. I remember how happy I was to see him coming. I had been given his name and had always been proud of it.

When Grandfather came within a few feet of me, he stopped. His stopping was an invitation for me to stop. Then — and this I would like the boys and girls and young people never to forget — he looked at me very earnestly and said:

"I would like to know what you have done with my name."

Everything I had ever done passed before me as if it were a flying picture on a screen — everything I had done. Quickly this vivid retrospect came down to the very time I was standing there. My whole life had passed before me. I smiled and looked at my grandfather and said:

"I have never done anything with your name of which you need be ashamed."

He stepped forward and took me in his arms, and as he did so, I became conscious again of my earthly surroundings. My pillow was as wet as if water had been poured on it — wet with tears of gratitude that I could answer unashamed.

I have thought of this many times, and I want to tell you that I have been trying, more than ever since that time, to take care of that name. So I want to say to the boys and girls, to the young men and women, to the youth of the Church and of all the world: Honor your fathers and your mothers. Honor the names that you bear, because some day you will have the privilege and the obligation of reporting to them (and to your Father in heaven) what you have done with their name.

Evil Spirits Rebuked

(Experience of Newel Knight)
(Taken from Scraps of Biography, page 66)

On the 14th of October, Brother Hyrum Smith and I held a meeting at my uncle Hezekiah Peek's. Brother Hyrum had great liberty of speech, and the Spirit of the Lord was poured out upon us in a miraculous manner. There was much good instruction and exhortation given, such as was calculated to encourage and strengthen the Saints in this their infantile state. At this meeting, four persons came forward and manifested their desire to forsake all, serve their God in humility, and obey the requirements of the gospel.

After the close of the meeting, Brother Hyrum and I intended going to spend the night with one of the brethren who lived a short distance from my uncle's, but as we were ready to start, the Spirit whispered to me that I should tarry there at my uncle's all night. I did so and retired to bed where I rested till midnight when my uncle came to my room and desired me to get up, saying he feared his wife was about to die. This surprised me as she was quite well when I went to bed. I dressed myself, and having asked my Heavenly Father to give me wisdom and power to rebuke the destroyer from the habitation, I went to the room where my aunt lay. She was in a most fearful condition; her eyes were closed; and she appeared to be in the last agonies of death. Presently she opened her eyes, and bade her husband and children farewell, telling them she must die for the redemption of this generation, as Jesus Christ had died for the generation in his day. Her whole frame shook, and she appeared to be racked with the most exquisite pain and torment. Her hands and feet were cold; and the blood settled in her fingers, while her husband and children stood weeping around her bed. This was a scene new to me and I felt she was suffering under the power of Satan — that was the same spirit that had bound and overpowered me at the time Joseph cast him out. I now cried unto the Lord for strength and wisdom that we might prevail over this wicked and delusive power. Just at this time my uncle cried aloud to me saying: "O, Brother Newel, cannot something be done?" I felt the Holy Spirit of the Lord rest upon me as he said this, and I immediately stepped forward, took her by the hand, and commanded Satan, in the name of the Lord Jesus Christ, to depart. I told my aunt she would not die but that she should live to see her children grow up, that Satan had deceived her and put a lying spirit in her mouth, that Christ had made the only and last atonement for all who would believe on his name, and that there should be no more shedding of blood for sin. She believed and stretched forth her hand, and cried unto me, and Satan departed from her.

A Child is Healed

(An experience of faith by Jacob Hamblin)

On the 15th of July, 1844, when taking leave of a small branch of the Church in Lightersburg, one of the sisters offered me some money that she had earned in the harvest field. I took one dollar and told her that I could get home with that.

After starting, I began to reflect on my situation. I must travel on the river steamers from Pittsburgh to Nauvoo, via Cincinnati and St. Louis, and I had only two dollars in my pocket. I had been often surprised when traveling on foot, at the pains people would take to invite me to ride or to step into a grocery and take a lunch, and I had considerable faith that the Lord would soften the heart of some one to assist me when I was in need.

When I arrived in Pittsburgh I had one dollar left. There were two steamers at the landing about to start for St. Louis. They offered to take passengers for a meager sum. I told the captain of one of them that I would give all the money I had for a passage to St. Louis. He took my money and gave me a ticket.

I was soon on my way down the river, but still a long way from home, and without money or anything to eat. I began to feel the want of food.

Nothing special occurred with me until evening when the lamps were lit in the passengers' cabin. I was then asked by a young married woman whether I was not a Mormon elder. I replied that I was. She told me that her little child was dying with the scarlet fever and wished me to lay hands on it and heal it.

I replied that I could administer to it and I presumed that the Lord would heal it. I asked her if she believed in such things. She said that she did and that she belonged to the Church but here husband did not. I was puzzled to know what to do for the boat was crowded with unbelievers, except for the mother of the sick child and me. It seemed like a special providence that just then the lamp in the cabin should fall from its hangings and leave us all in the dark.

Before another lamp could be lit, I had administered to the child and rebuked the fever in the name of the Lord Jesus, unobserved by those around. The Lord blessed the administration, and the child was healed.

The mother called her husband, and said to him, "Little Mary is healed; now do not say anything against Mormonism." The man looked at his child, and said to me, "I am not a believer in any kind of religion, but I am on my way to Iowa, opposite to Nauvoo, where I presume you are going. You are welcome to board with me all the way, and if you want any money I will let you have it."

Healing at Commerce

(Excerpts from *H. C. Kimball's Journal* published by
Juvenile Instructor Office, 1882)

A great amount of sickness prevailed
among the inhabitants of Commerce in consequence of the sufferings and hardships to
which they had been subjected in being driv-
en from Missouri. Those who were able to
be about spent their time in administering to
the sick. Some had faith and were healed.
To those who had no faith we administered
mild herbs and nursed them as well as possible under the circumstances, but many died.

One morning, the Prophet Joseph Smith
arose from his bed of sickness when the power
of God rested upon him, and went forth ad-
miinstering to the sick. He commenced with
the sick in his own house, then visited those
who were tenting in his dooryard, commanding the sick in the name of the Lord Jesus
Christ to arise from their beds and be made
whole, and they were healed according to his
words. He then went from house to house and
from tent to tent on the bank of the river,
healing the sick by the power of Israel's God
as he went among them. He did not miss a

single house, wagon, or tent, and continued
this work up to the "Upper Stone House,"
where he crossed the river, accompanied by
P. P. Pratt, O. Pratt, John Taylor, John E.
Page and me. He walked into the cabin of
Brother Brigham Young, who was lying very
sick, and commanded him in the name of the
Lord Jesus to arise and be made whole. He
arose, healed of his sickness, and accompanied Joseph and his brethren of the Twelve.
They went into the house of Brother Elijah
Fordham, who was insensible and considered
by his family and friends to be dying. Joseph
stepped to his bedside, looked him in the eye
for a minute without speaking then took him
by the hand and commanded him in the name
of Jesus Christ to arise from his bed and
walk. Brother Fordham instantly leaped out
of his bed, threw off all his poultices and
bandages, dressed himself, called for a bowl
of bread and milk, which he ate, and then
followed us into the street.

We then went into the house of Joseph
B. Noble, who was also very sick, and he
was healed in the same manner.

Joseph spoke with the voice and power
of God.

When he had healed all the sick by the power given unto him, he went down to the ferryboat, when a stranger rode up almost breathless and said he had heard "Jo" Smith raising the dead and healing all the sick, and his wife begged of him to ride up and get Mr. Smith to go down and heal his twin children, who were about five months old. Joseph replied, "I cannot go but will send someone." In a few minutes he said to Elder Woodruff, who lived in Montrose. "You go and heal those children. Take this pocket handkerchief, and when you administer to them, wipe their faces with it, and they shall recover." Brother Woodruff did as he was commanded, and the children were healed.

When the mob leaders saw men who they thought were dying arise from their beds and pray for others, they stood paralyzed with fear. Yet those same men would have killed Joseph and his brethren if they had had an opportunity.

Joseph recrossed the river and returned to his own house, and I went to my home, rejoicing in the mercies and goodness of God.

This was a day never to be forgotten by the Saints, nor by the wicked, for they saw the power of God manifest in the flesh.

A Lieutenant's Courage

(An incident which was written by Elder Hugh B.
Brown, of the Council of the Twelve)

It is not always necessary to go to a battle-field to display one's courage or bravery. Here is a short story of a lieutenant in the Canadian army who had the moral courage to stand for what he knew was right, even at the risk of displeasing his commanding officer.

This young man had been recommended to take the officers' training course and for this purpose went to Sarcee Camp near Calgary, Alberta. He was timid when he first went on parade and was very anxious to make a good impression and to please his officers.

After the first drill his captain, knowing he was from Cardston and thinking he was therefore a Mormon, asked the young man and two other lieutenants to go with him to his tent. Sitting down at his desk he asked the other officers to be seated, and he poured some liquor in some glasses and passed it to the young officers. As he offered the Mormon boy a drink he said, "I see you are a bit strange and awkward here, and I think a drink of liquor wil make you feel more at home."

For a moment the boy hesitated as he was very anxious to please his captain, but remembering his Sunday School song, "Do What Is Right, Let the Consequence Follow", he politely said, "Thank you, sir, but I do not drink." "Oh," said the captain, "so you do not drink. Well then, have a cigar," and he passed a box of cigars to the three of them. "I am sorry, sir, to seem rude, but I do not smoke," said the boy. The captain seemed to be quite angry. He swore and said, "So you do not smoke and you do not drink. Well, what kind of soldier do you think you will make?" With that he left the tent abruptly.

The two lieutenants turned on the boy and said, "You young fool. Don't you know it is a very unusual thing for a captain to offer to treat a lieutenant to a drink or smoke. He was trying to make you feel at home. You were rude enough to refuse him. You'll never be much of an officer unless you learn at least to be polite."

The boy replied, "If I have to smoke and drink to be a good officer, I guess I'll have to

be a private. I am preparing to defend my
country, and I think one must be honest with
himself to be truly patriotic."

Some months later at the close of the term
of training, the young officers were assembled
for an examination and the captain was in
charge. They were in a large tent called a
Marquee and the chairs were spaced so that
it was impossible for anyone to see another's
paper. Just as the questions were being dis-
tributed, the captain asked the lieutenant if
he would go on an errand to Calgary for him
and write his examination when he returned.

It was dusk when he returned to camp and
time for mess, so he reported to the captain
at his headquarters tent and was told to eat
first and then come back for the examination.
When he returned, the captain handed him the
examination questions and told him to sit
at his desk and write the answers. The captain said he was going to town, but the lieutenant could write the answers and leave them
on the desk.

"But, sir," said the lieutenant, "all of the
textbooks are here on this desk, and I should
not be left alone to write. I could get all of the

answers out of these books." "You could, but you won't," said the captain. "A man who has the courage you had the first time we met and is honest enough to do what he knows he should do when none of his relatives or home folks are watching will not cheat even if left alone at a teacher's desk."

Five years later this captain, who was then a lieutenant colonel, was in France in the first world war and the young lieutenant, now a captain, was in his battalion. One night a message came from the general asking the colonel to recommend a trusted officer to undertake a dangerous mission into enemy territory. The message further said, "We must have a man who has moral courage and will not break even if he is captured and tortured by the enemy."

Immediately the colonel remembered the young lieutenant who was with him in Alberta and he recommended him for the difficult mission. He was interviewed by the general, told what his duties were, and sent on his way. He returned and reported to the general a few days later and was highly commended for being an outstanding Canadian officer.

The world needs men of courage and virtue to face the hazards and uncertainties of the future. Be true and loyal to yourself, and then, whether you are a subject of a "king, president, ruler, or magistrate" you will be a credit to your country and will "obey, honor, and sustain the law."

Determined to Keep the Sabbath

(Brother O. H. Snow tells an interesting experience he
had as a young man just after he
returned from his mission)

It so happened that my mission ended when Grover Cleveland was President of the United States. The country was passing through one of its worst depressions. Work was hard to find. I came back home in debt. My mother had been a widow since I was ten years of age. It was very necessary that I find some kind of work to assist her. I also desired to get a little something to begin making a home for myself. Father had left mother with but very little property, and it was not possible for Mother to give further aid after my mission expenses weer met.

It was about this time that the new mining camp of DeLamar, Nevada, was opened up. Some of the boys went out to find work, and were able to get contracts to haul· wood to a smelter that was being built.

In company with some members of the ward, I went out to the new camp and we soon took a contract to deliver five hundred cords of wood. We hired choppers and began work. When the week ended and Sunday morning rolled around, I rose early, watered and fed my team, and turned them loose on the hillside to graze.

When our foreman saw what I had done, he asked what it meant. I said, "It is Sunday."

He asked, "Don't you intend to haul wood?"

I replied, "No."

He then said, "We are going to get our loads."

"I said, "That's all right, but I'm not." He argued and the other boys joined in saying that we were in a mining camp. I told them that I had been out teaching others who lived outside of Mormon communities Sabbath observance along with other gospel truths and that I could not conscientiously work on Sunday. I felt the Lord meant the Sabbath as much for a mining camp as for any other place.

Our foreman then gave the ultimatum that if I would not work on Sunday we should have to pile our wood separately. I said that was all right, that we could measure up what was already in and I would begin next day to pile my wood in a different place.

The next day I moved camp about a quarter of a mile away went to town with my load of wood and found two acquaintances hunting work. I hired them to chop my wood for me and assist me in loading and cleaning up the timber.

We continued to work for about four months to complete our contract. I lost only two half days during the summer, one for resetting my wagon tires, and the other when I changed camps and found my wood choppers. I rested each Sunday, spending the time reading good books. I made twelve trips each week, with two exceptions, after I left the other boys while they made but ten trips, and made more misses than I did by reason of some accidents. My team was fatter, I was much less worn and when we settled up, my average monthly earnings were approximately twenty-five dollars a month in excess of those of my former partners.

*

Rather be a Deacon

In a conversation with Dr. Haymond, James A. Farley, Postmaster General under President Franklin Delano Roosevelt, said: "I am a Democrat of some national prominence, and Reed Smoot is a Republican; but I consider him to be the greatest diplomat in the United States Government. He knows more of what is going on, attends more meetings, and is a better authority on all that goes on than anyone else I know. I wish we had more men exactly like him.

"I have been reliably informed that Reed Smoot was offered the nomination for the Presidency of the United States, on the Republican ticket, if he would deny his faith — his being a Mormon would make it impossible for him to receive any such nomination."

Dr. Haymond continued: "Fifteen years later, Senator Smoot was in my office and during the conversation, I told him what James Farley had told me. He said: "In two national Republican Conventions, I was offered the nomination for President of the United States, if I could turn against my Church."

"I said to him: 'Wouldn't it be worth it?'

"He whirled on me, took me by the arm and said: 'Young man, maybe you do not know my stand in regard to my Church. If I had to take my choice of being a deacon in the Church of Jesus Christ of Latter-day Saints, or being the President of the United States, I would be a deacon.'"

An Answered Prayer

(An experience where God provided for
Jacob Hamblin's family)

I labored with the company of pioneers to prepare the way for the Saints through Iowa, after which I had the privilege of returning to Nauvoo for my family, which consisted of my wife and three children. I moved them out into Iowa, 200 miles, where I left them, and returned 100 miles to settments, in order to obtain food and other necessaries.

I was taken sick, and sent for my family to return to me. My wife and two children were taken sick the day after their arrival. We found shelter in a miserable hut, some distance from water.

One day I made an effort to get some water for my suffering family but failed through weakness. Night came on, and my family were burning with fever and calling for water.

These very trying circumstances called up some bitter feelings within me. It seemed as if in this, my terrible extremity, the Lord permitted the devil to try me, for just then a Methodist class leader came along, and remarked that I was in a very bad situation. He assured me that he had a comfortable house that I could move into, that he had plenty of everything, and would assist me if I would renounce Mormonism. I refused, and he passed on.

I afterwards knelt down and asked the Lord to pity us in our miserable condition, and to soften the heart of someone to administer to us in our affliction.

About an hour after this, a man by the name of William Johnson came with a three-gallon jug full of water, set it down and said: "I came home this evening, weary, having been working with a threshing machine during the day, but when I lay down, I could not sleep; something told me that you were suffering for water. I took this jug, went over to Custer's well and got this for you. I feel now as if I could go home and sleep. If you need anything else I will let you have it.' I knew this was from the Lord in answer to my prayer.

The following day the quails came out of the thickets and were so easily caught that

I picked up what I needed without difficulty. I afterwards learned that the camps of the Saints had been supplied with food in the same way.

ↄ

A Story of Two Boys

A number of years ago I went into the County Hospital in Salt Lake City for the purpose of administering to the sick. Lying on a bed was a boy nine years old, a charity patient of whom I had heard. He was emaciated and had pneumonia, among other things. I said, "Lawrence, do you feel very sick?"

He answered, "Yes."

"I said "Have you suffered much pain?"

"Awful pain," he replied.

I said, "Have you asked the Lord to take the pain away?"

"The little fellow looked up in amazement and said, "I don't know how."

He had never been taught to pray. He had never been taught that there is a power greater than man's power. I explained to him that he could ask the Lord to bless him. Then we asked the Lord to bless him.

I asked myself this question: "How many homes are there were husband and wife, father and mother, understand the gospel? How many children growing up in those homes do not know how to pray?"

A few days after that, I heard of another nine-year-old boy, an orphan, who was hurried off to the hospital where examination indicated that he had to be operated upon without delay. He had been living with friends who had given him a home. His father and mother (when they were alive) had taught him to pray. Thus, when he came to the hospital, the thing he wanted was to have the Lord help him.

The doctors had decided to hold a consultation. When he was wheeled into the operating room, he looked around and saw the nurses and the doctors who had consulted on his case. He knew that it was very serious and he said to one of them as they were preparing to give him the anesthetic: "Doctor, before you begin to operate, won't you please pray for me?"

The doctor, with seeming embarrassment, offered his excuses and said, "I can't pray for you." Then the boy asked the other doctors, with the same result.

Finally, something very remarkable happened. This little fellow said, "If you can't pray for me, will you please wait while I pray for myself?"

They removed the sheet, and he knelt on the operating table, bowed his head and said, "Heavenly Father, I am only an orphan boy. I am awful sick. Won't you please make me well? Bless these men who are going to operate that they will do it right. If you will, make me well I will try to grow up to be a good man. Thank you, Heavenly Father, for making me well."

When he got through praying, he lay down. The doctors' and the nurses' eyes filled with tears. Then he said, "I am ready."

Th operation was performed. The little fellow was taken back to his room and in a few days they took him from the hospital, well on the way to complete recovery.

Some days after that a man who had heard of the incident went to the office of one of the surgeons and said, "Tell me about the operation you performed a few days ago — the operation on a little boy."

The surgeon said, "I have operated on several little boys."

The man added, "This little boy wanted someone to pray for him."

The doctor said very seriously, "There was such a case but I don't know but that it is too sacred a thing for me to talk about."

The man said, "Doctor, if you will tell me, I will treat it with respect. I would like to hear it."

Then the doctor told the story about as I have told it here, and added: "I have operated on hundreds of people, men and women, who thought they had faith to be healed. But never until I stood over that little boy have I felt the presence of God as I felt it then. That boy opened the windows of heaven and talked to his Heavenly Father as one would talk to another face to face. I want to say to you that I am a better man for having had this experience of standing and hearing a little boy talk to his Father in Heaven as if he were present."

"Remember there is a God in heaven — and parents ... shall ... teach their children to pray, and to walk uprightly before the Lord." (D.&C. 68:28)

In the Hour of Parting

(By President Heber J. Grant)

It is the purpose of God, that the body and the spirit shall be eternally united and that there will come a time, through the blessing and mercy of God, when we will no more have sorrow but when we shall have conquered all of these things that are of a trying and distressing character, and shall stand up in the presence of the living God, filled with joy and peace and satisfaction.

I was thoroughly convinced in my own mind and in my own heart, when my first wife left me by death, that it was the will of the Lord that she should be called away. I bowed in humility at her death. The Lord saw fit upon that occasion to give to one of my little children a testimony that the death of her mother was the will of the Lord.

About one hour before my wife died, I called my children into her room and told them that either mother was dying and for them to bid her goodbye. One of the little girls, about twelve years of age, said to me: "Papa, I do not want my Mamma to die. I have been with you in the hospital in San Francisco for six months; time and time again when Mamma was in distress you have administered to her and she has been relieved of her pain and quietly gone to sleep. I want you to lay hands upon my Mamma and heal her."

I told my little girl that we all had to die sometime and that I felt assured in my heart that her mother's time had arrived; and she and the rest of the children left the room.

I then knelt down by the bed of my wife (who by this time had lost consciousness) and I told the Lord I acknowledged His hand in life, in death, in joy, in sorrow, in prosperity or adversity; I thanked Him for the knowledge I had that my wife belonged to me for all eternity, that the Gospel of Jesus Christ had been restored, that I knew that by the power and authority of the Priesthood here on the earth that I could and would have my wife forever if I were only faithful as she had been; but I told the Lord that I lacked the strength to have my wife die and to have it affect the faith of my little children in the ordinances of the Gospel of Jesus Christ; and I supplicated the Lord with all the strength that I possessed, that He would give to that little girl of mine a knowledge that it was His mind and His will that her Mamma should die.

Within an hour my wife passed away, and I called the children back into the room. My little boy about five and a half or six years of age was weeping bitterly, and the little girl twelve years of age took him in her arms and said: "Do not weep, do not cry, Heber; since we went out of this room the voice of the Lord from heaven has said to me, 'In the death of your Mamma the will of the Lord shall be done.'"

Tell me, my friends, that I do not know that God hears and answers prayers! Tell me that I do not know that in the hour of adversity the Latter-day Saints are comforted and blessed and consoled as no other people are!

Off the Shores of Kwajalein

(Off the Shores of Kwajalein, Honolulu, February 8, 1944, United Press)

Some folks say that the day of miracles has passed. Some people say that such things as this just don't happen, yet here's a story which will leave you breathless and wondering — for it concerns two inconspicuous boys of the United States Marine Corps and the battle for the Marshall Islands.

The time was just before dawn when the great gray hulks of battleships lay against the cool horizon of the blue Pacific. Aboard those ships the boys were anxiously awaiting the first signal which would announce the start of the drive to take one of the greatest

of Japanese bases, Kwajalein Atoll. The duties
of the men aboard the big ships would require
the rather remote but strenuous work of bom-
bardment. It was the men on the smaller
boats, who must wade through the final
stretch of water and brave the withering fire
of the murderous Japanese machine guns.
Slowly the minutes ticked by into what seemed hours. Actually the time was twenty minutes to six when the final word came. From
over the horizon tons of shells began pouring
into the Japanese positions from the big ships.
It seemed that all hell broke loose, for Kwajalein began to heave and surge with a convul-
sive shock of death. A star-flare lit the sky,
and the smaller boats began pouring out the
men who were destined to take the island.
From far above, barely audible at first, then
building into a roaring crescendo, allied bomb-
ers dove toward the ground, blowing ad-
jacent buildings to bits. Slowly toward shore
the men of the United States Marines edged
closer and closer. In a moment they would be
sighted by the Japanese. In a moment, bullets
would begin spattering around them from
pillboxes skilfully hidden on the beach. But,

on they came, and soon the battle was joined by the men whose glory is destined to be written in the annals of history. The splatter of machine guns soon laid a death pattern on the men wading toward shore. Here and there they went down, some wounded, some dead — and it is about two of these wounded that we speak of at the moment. The battle went on and the men of the Marine Corps — despite the wounds and death of their comrades — went in.

Being a war correspondent, my boat was going in behind the first line of men, and we came upon these two wounded Marines in the water. One, from the stain of red around him, we could tell, was badly wounded; the other, wounded too, was holding the other boy's head above water. We picked them up midst a hail of shots from shore then pulled back toward safer retreat to render first aid. The one boy seemed too far gone to need much help, but the other boy refused aid until his wounded buddy was attended. But our help seemed insufficient, as we soon realized, and we announced our decision to his comrade. Then it happened.

This young man, bronzed by the tropical sun, clean as a shark's tooth in the South Seas, slowly got to his knees. His one arm was nearly gone, but the other, he lifted the head of his uncosncious buddy into his lap, placed his good hand on the other's pale brow and uttered what to us seemed to be incredible words — words which to this moment are emblazoned in unforgettable letters across the doorway of my memory: "In the Name of Jesus Christ and by virtue of the Holy Priesthood which I hold, I command you to remain alive until the necessary help can be obtained to secure the preservation of your life."

Today the three of us are here in Honolulu, and he is still alive. In fact, we walked down the beach together today, as we convalesce. He is the wonder of the Medical Unit for they say he should be dead. Why he isn't they don't know — but we do, for we were there, off the shores of KWAJALEIN!

Samuel Blue's Triumph

(Excerpt of Brother SAMUEL "THUNDERHEAD"
BLUE, South Carolina Ca-ta-ba Indian LDS brother.
Bro. Blue born 15 August 1872, joined the Church
at age of 12, is an Indian Chief)

Important to Brother Blue are the powers
of the priesthood and the authority that ac-
companies the servants of the Lord. He relates
the following experiences and bears witness
to the truthfulness of the gospel and its promises.

One day my nine-year-old son (Joseph
Harvey) went hunting with six other Indians.
They were hunting squirrels. A squirrel darted
up a pine tree, and my son climbed up the
tree to scare him out on a limb. Finally the
squirrel ran out on a branch. My son called
to the hunters to hold their fire until he could
get down out of the tree. Two of the Indians,
however, shot a father and his son. They had
always acted jealously of me and of my family because I was the chief. They deliberately
shot at my boy. He was filled with buckshot
from his knees to the top of his head. One
blast was aimed at his groin and the other
hit him squarely in the face. The Indians

carried my boy toward our home and found a cool spot along the trail under a pine tree. There they laid him down and ran for a doctor.

A friend came to me in Rock Hills where I had gone to buy groceries, and said, "Sam, run home at once, your boy has been shot!" I thought it was one of my married sons. I left my team and wagon in town, and drove home with the doctor and found my baby boy near death. He (the doctor) put the boy to sleep with some morphine so he wouldn't feel the pain. He said my boy could not live. He died in a few minutes.

The man (the father) who had done the shooting had locked his son up to protect him, and he had come over to my house to visit the crowd who had gathered to offer their help. He did not appear to be very upset at his deed. My heart filled with revenge and hatred, and I reached for my double-barreled shotgun. My wife and my mother stopped me. Someone brought me a telegram that had been sent by President Callis from Atlanta, Georgia, the mission headquarters. The telegram said, 'Don't do anything until I see you. I am coming. — Charles A. Callis."

I read the telegram but revenge was all I could think about. Something seemed to whisper to me, "If you don't take down your gun and kill the man who murdered your son, Sam Blue, you are a coward."

Now I had been a Mormon ever since I was a young lad, and I knew it would not be right to take revenge. I decided to pray to the Lord about it. I left the house and walked to a secret place out in the timber where I always go to pray when I have an important problem, and there I prayed to the Lord to take revenge out of my heart. I soon felt better and started back to the house.

As I approached the house I heard something whisper to me, "Sam Blue, you are a coward if you don't kill that Indian." I turned and went back to pray. This time I had to pray longer before I felt better. On my way back to the house, at the same spot along the path, I heard the voice say again, "Sam Blue, you are a coward if you don't kill the man who murdered your son." I turned again and went back to pray. This time I told the Lord he must help me or I would kill. I asked him to take revenge out of my heart and keep it out. I felt good when I got up from praying. I went back to the house and when I reached the house and shook hands with the Indian who killed my boy — there was no hatred or desire for revenge in my heart.

President Callis arrived the next day and comforted me. He had lost two of his little boys here in the south. He said he knew when I was in trouble, and so he sent the telegram and took the first train that left Atlanta to come to me.

The first thing that President Callis said to me were the words of the Saviour, "Vengeance is mine and I will repay." He asked me what I had done, and I told him, and he told me I was right. As he left he shook hands with me and pressed a fifty dollar bill into my hand with the suggestion that I use it to help bear the expense.

Since that time I have often said President Callis was my Savior — he saved me from being a murderer and ruining my life. Of course, I don't mean any reflection on the Master who is really the Savior of us all.

Saved from a Mob

(Excerpts from *Labors in the Vineyard*, published at
Juvenile Instructor Office, 1884)

(From section titled THE LORD'S BLESS-
INGS.) The following account of the Lord's
blesings is related by Amasa Potter:

In the spring of 1856, in the days of my
youth, I was called by the First Presidency
of the Church of Jesus Christ of Latter-day
Saints to go on a mission to Australia to
preach the gospel. When we came to the city
called Camden, forty miles from Sydney, we
concluded to try to get a place to preach in.
We were refused all public houses that we
asked for. Finally we tried to get the privilege of stopping at a public house, or tavern,
all night. We told the landlord that we were
missionaries of the Church of Jesus Christ
of Latter-day Saints, and we were traveling
without purse or scrip, according to the pattern that Jesus had left on record in the
Bible. The landlord asked us if we were Mormons. We said that we were called that name
by the world. After talking some time with
him he ordered us out of the house and told

some drunken Irishmen to run us out of town
and he would give them a gallon of rum each.
It was now after dark, and we went down
one of the streets and called at a large boot
and shoe shop. The owner said he would keep
us, and we were having a good discussion on
the principles of the gospel when a rough
voice called to the master of the place and
said,

"Are you going to keep them d----d Mormons here all night?"

We looked towards the door and saw there
a mob of drunnken men, armed with native
war clubs, spears, and the boomerangs. The
boomerang is a weapon with which the natives
formerly fought.

I said to my companion, "We must get out
of here."

He replied, "How shall we do it without
getting hurt?"

I told him that God had not sent us here
to be killed in this manner, and if we would
now trust wholly in the Lord, he would deliver us.

I had no more than said these words when
the owner of the house caught the same spirit

as the mob and said to us, "Get out of my house, or I will kill you," and, at the same time, struck at my partner with a hammer, but missed him as he sprang to one side.

The mob said, "Drive them out, and we will use them up in a hurry."

I picked up my carpetbag and umbrella and went to the door with a prayerful heart to God that he would protect us, and I walked out between many of them. It appeared that they did not see me or they did not notice me. The mob was arranged on both sides of the door, with their weapons drawn ready to strike at the first sight of us, and as my partner came out the leader of the band called the attention of his men to give some instructions how to deal with us, and thus he slipped past them unseen. I took him by the arm, and we started down the street. In the darkness of the night they could not see us. About this time the owner of the house came to the door and they asked him where the Mormons were. He replied that they had gone out just that minute. They said they knew better, "for," said they, "they have not passed us, and you had better bring them out, or we will knock your house down." At that they broke into the house and, not finding us, they took the master and journeyman out and beat them almost to death.

In this deliverance, the prediction of President Heber C. Kimball was fulfilled; for he said that I should be brought into many close places, and it would seem that death stared me in the face; but, if I would be faithful to my mission, the angels of God would deliver me in all trials, and I should return in safety to the Church and to my home.

The Retreat

The spring of 1940 was unlike any other spring in Switzerland. Instead of bringing joy and happiness in the wake of the newly awakened nature and all of its magnificent glory, it brought news of bloodshed and persecution, starvation, destruction, and other horrors accompanying the first year of World War II.

But even more than that, it brought with it the constant fear of being invaded by the

German army and losing that divine gift of
freedom which is more precious than life, a
gift the Swiss people had enjoyed for many
centuries. Day after day, rumors of expected
attacks caused deep concern and anxiety
among the Swiss. In the hearts of the thousands of refugees who had fled into this little
peaceful land of Switzerland there was an
agonizing fear.

One night, just before retiring, Max Zimmer, who was presiding over the Swiss Mission, received a confidential telephone call
from a member of the L.D.S. Church who had
an important position in the Swiss Army. He
was told that the German army at that moment was advancing toward the Swiss border
and that the Swiss troops were ready for action on a minute's notice.

Fear for one's own life was overshadowed
by the great concern for one's country. Switzerland has been a haven for the persecuted
and had become the symbol of freedom.

Similar thoughts must have been in President Zimmer's mind as he called his family
together for prayer. In great humility and

with unshakeable faith in God and his power, he pleaded with the Lord not to allow this power of darkness to crush the flame of freedom that had been kindled carefully by the Swiss throughout the centuries and was now being carried proudly by them in these troublesome war days.

As a bearer of the Holy Priesthood he covenanted with the Lord that if he would intervene, Elder Zimmer would consecrate his life to his work and bear testimony of his power.

He remembered the thousands of refugees who had come into Switzerland during the past few years to continue their underground activities for the cause of liberty and the right to worship God according to the dictates of their conscience. Most of that night he prayed unto the Lord with all his heart, humbly stating, "Thy will be done."

As the gloomy darkness of the night gave way to the first faint light of dawn, the family was still kneeling in humble prayer when the phone rang, piercing the silence of the room.

The message was that for some miraculous reason the German army had retreated after having advanced to a very short distance from the Swiss-German border.

✍

You May Come Back

There is a story told of a manager of one of the largest manufacturing plants in the United States, who was known as a rather reserved, quiet, but most efficient executive. One day a factory superintendent sought the manager in his office, and was told by the secretary, who sat in the outer office, that the manager was "in conference" and "was not to be disturbed."

"But how can he be in conference?" There is nobody in the office but himself," expostulated the superintendent, an impetuous sort of man.

He had seen the manager enter the office alone. "I must see him on a matter of great importance." He pushed by the secretary even after she said. "You may come back in a few moments, at present he is not to be disturbed."

When the superintendent opened the door to the manager's private office, he gave a quick glance and quietly closed the door. "Why, he is on his knees!"

"Yes, in conference as I told you," said the secretary.

You Will Get Those Arms

(Taken from Scraps of Biography, page 33)

I will mention one prophecy among the many predictions of the Prophet Joseph Smith that was literally fulfilled.

During the persecutions in the fall of 1838, one of the brethren happened to be a stranger in Richmond, Ray Co., Missouri, a distance of some thirty or forty miles from Far West, in Caldwell County, where the Saints dwelt. About sundown he saw men loading guns into a carriage and learned that they were to be taken that night to the mob in Daviess County to fight the Mormons. He feigned to be traveling in the opposite direction and took a circuitous route to Far West, arriving there about eight o'clock the next morning. He related what he had seen of the actions of the mob and a call was immediately made for ten volunteers to accompany Captain Allred of the militia to intercept and take the arms. To do this we had about twenty miles to ride across a trackless prairie to reach the road leading from Richmond to Daviess County where the mob was quartered. The man with the guns had a good, smooth road, free from rocks or obstructions of any kind, and to all human appearance, might have reached his destination before we obtained the news of his having the arms.

When all were mounted the Prophet Joseph said to Brother Allred, "I want you to ride as fast as your horses can carry you, and you will get those arms." These last words inspired faith in the little band and even the horses did not seem to become weary.

When we neared the road, we cast our eyes towards Richmond and at a distance of about half a mile we discovered a black-covered carriage standing in the road without any team attached to it. On nearing it, we saw that it was empty. We examined and found that one of the axles was newly broken in two. Here was the carriage described, but where were the guns? We soon discovered a trail in the high grass where something heavy had been dragged from the carriage. We followed this trail a short distance and found a wooden box containing seventy-four United States yaugers. While consulting how to get them to the town, we looked in the direction of the mob and discovered two men coming about as fast as they could drive in a lumber wagon. When they discovered us, they supposed us to be mobs and swung their hats and shouted "hurrah!" two or three times. Our little troop responded in the same way.

They got very near before they discovered their mistake. Brother Allred directed the teamster to drive alongside of the box. He then told the two men to get out and put it into the wagon and then follow him. We returned the way we came, and reached our destination about sundown. After the guns were taken from the wagon, the men and team were released. The prediction of the Prophet was fulfilled and the long-range guns, which were the best then known, were in our hands.

Joseph, knowing that the guns were government property, sent a dispatch immediately to notify General Atchinson and Colonel Doniphan of Clay County what had been done. They directed that the arms should be delivered over to them, and pledged their honor that they should not be used against our people.

The Prophet's patriotism would not allow him to retain government property although it had been obtained by our enemies for our destruction. If this was not a test of loyalty, I fail to see an opportunity where a test could be given.

Part Two

A Son's Letter

(Excerpt of a Sermon by an unknown Author)

Dear Dad:

I am writing this to you, though you have been dead thirty years.

From your seat in the Place Beyond I hope you can see these lines. I feel I must say some things to you, things I didn't know when I was a boy in your house, things I was too stupid to say.

It's only now, after passing through the long, hard school of years; only now, when my own hair is gray, that I understand how you felt.

I must have been a bitter trial to you. I was such a fool. I believed my own petty wisdom, and I know how ridiculous it was, compared to that calm, ripe, wholesome wisdom of yours.

Most of all I want to confess my worst sin against you. It was the feeling I had that you "did not understand."

When I look back over it now, I know that you did understand. You understood me better than I did myself. Your wisdom flowed around mine like the ocean around an island.

And how patient you were with me! How full of long-suffering and kindness.

And how pathetic, it now comes to me, were your efforts to get close to me, to win my confidence, to be my pal!

I wouldn't let you. I couldn't. What was it held me aloof? I don't know. But it was tragic — that wall that rises between a boy and his father, and their frantic attempts to see through it and climb over it.

I wish you were here now, across the table from me just for an hour, so that I could tell you how there's no wall any more; I understand you now, Dad, and God knows how I love you and how I wish I could go back to be your boy again.

I know now how I could make you happy every day. I know how you felt.

Well, it won't be long, Dad, till I am over, and I believe you'll be the first to take me by the hand and take me up the further slope.

And I'll put in the first thousand years or so making you realize that not one pang or yearning you spent on me was wasted. It took a good many years for this prodigal son — and all sons are in a measure prodigal — to come to himself, but I've come. I see it all now.

I know that the richest, most priceless thing on earth, and the thing least understood, is that mighty love and tenderness and craving to help which a father feels toward his boy. For I have a boy of my own.

And it is he that makes me want to go back to you and get down on my knees to you.

Up there somewhere in the silence, hear me, Dad, and believe me.

A Style of Our Own

(Excerpt from an extemporaneous address given at B.Y.U. University by Elder Spencer Kimball February 13, 1951)

What is the *most dear and precious above all things?* It is chastity and virtue! What is the greatest, the most abominable sin in the world which comes in the lives of people generally? It is the sin of adultery. It deprives them of that which is the most dear and precious thing above all things: chastity and virtue.

The world has come a long way from the doctrine of body and soul cleanliness. Unchastity, sexual impurity, have come to be the order of the day. High school girls and boys, and college boys and girls, are falling prey to this insidious sin which can keep them from their Heavenly Father. I know this to be true. I am not talking about something, my young brothers and sisters, of which I do not know. With others of the Brethren I interview thousands of young people and older folks for advancement in priesthood orders, to go on missions and as officers of the Church. And while we find great numbers of our members are clean and virtuous, we do find all too many who have had serious moral problems. We feel certain that there is no people as nearly free from this taint; yet live in the world, and the world has defiled too great a number.

Unchastity is the great demon of the day! Avoid it, young people, as you would the

smallpox, the leprosy and, as you would the
direst calamities.

On Sinai God wrote on the tablets: "Thou
shalt not kill. Thou shalt not commit adultery." In one breath he said it — "Thou shalt
not kill. Thou shalt not commit adultery."
Did he not mean thereby that the second was
little, if any, behind the first? It is most important that we understand and know the
seriousness of these sins.

A young couple came to me some time ago
desiring to be married in the temple. From
the day of their engagement six months earlier
they had been unchaste. Six months of unchastity, and when I discussed it with them
they said (and you'll hardly believe this):
"Well, that isn't so very wrong, is it Brother
Kimball?" I shuddered. Is it possible that any
Latter-day Saint boy or girl could have arrived at marriageable age and not know that
this evil is the most abominable sin next to
the shedding of innocent blood and the denying of the Holy Ghost, which latter few of us
could do? I was shocked when I saw they
were serious. "That isn't so very wrong, is
it?" they asked. How do you reach such con-

clusions? How can your defenses and rationalizations lead you so far away? "But we were engaged and expected to be married," they countered. Since when did God open the door to engaged youth to commit fornication? What makes you think that intended marriage is a coverall for such sins? How can engagement reduce the sin of sexual indulgence?

I think there are many things which lead us to that attitude. I'm going to tell you some of the situations, which break down our moral structures. Some get careless and inactive. The Gospel isn't quite so important to them. They fail to attend meetings. They let school work, social life, or business, or professions come in and crowd out the important Church activities and the Gospel, until finally they do not feel quite so keenly their responsibilities and are not so enthusiastic.

One contributing factor to immodesty and a breakdown of moral values is the modern dress. I know I'm not going to be popular when I say this, but I am sure that the immodest dresses that are worn by our young women, and their mothers, contribute in some degree to the immorality of this age. Even

some of our mothers, wives and sisters wear
low-neck dresses, and wear and encourage the
wearing of other immodest clothes even strap
and strapless evening gowns by their youth.
Even fathers sometime encourage it. I wonder if our young sisters realize the temptation they are flaunting before young men
when they leave their bodies partly uncovered.
I wonder! I notice frequently the very tight-
fitting sweaters, body-revealing, form-fitting
sweaters which seem to be worn to emphasize
the form of the girl who wears them.

I see young women on the streets wearing shorts. If there is any appropriate place
for women to wear shorts it is in their own
rooms, in their own homes. They are immodest. President George Albert Smith, our
Prophet, has mentioned this many times. He
said to us, "Brethren, when you go out into
the stakes, preach modesty." And so I am
imploring you to be modest.

I see in the papers constantly, things that
hurt me. These queen contests have become
common. It seems that every class, every
group, every club, must have a queen. The
flattery resulting is frequently destructive to

the queen. If I had a hundred daughters I would resist any one's ever becoming a queen, the object of a beauty parade or contest. Here's a quote from a Salt Lake City newspaper: "Judging of contestants is based on personality, appearance in an evening gown, appearance in a bathing suit, and talent."

Now let me say a word about the "appearance in an evening gown." Evening gowns can be most beautiful and modest if they clothe the body. But the Lord never did intend that they should be backless or topless. Now, I want to tell you, it leads to sin.

There is no reason why any woman needs to wear a gown just because it is the worldly style. We can create a style of our own. I know women who have worn many evening gowns and have never yet worn an immodest one, and they have purchased them from the stores. And any store, I believe, in any area, will stock the dresses that the trade demands. I went to a function once, a university ball. Two-thirds of all the young women who came to that dance came in strapless gowns or with strap gowns and there is very little difference. They are an abomination in the sight of

the Lord. I do not know what our mothers
are thinking, who will let their young daughters wear gowns that are immodest. I repeat
again — you do not realize, I am sure, how
much temptation you are flaunting before a
young man. Now, a woman is most beautiful
when her body is clothed and her sweet face
adorned with her lovely hair. She needs no
more attractions. Then she is at her best,
and men will love her for it. And men will
not love her more because her neck or back is
bare. Girls, if he is decent and worthy of you
he will love you more when you are properly
dressed! Of course, if he is a vicious man,
he would like you to be dressed only par-
tially.

Now, another quote: "Ten finalists in the
Miss .... contest Wednesday night, will
make their last talent and beauty parade
before the eyes of the judges and crowds at
the State Fair." "Just how good a figure does
Miss .... have? That's a question that may
be settled without difficulty Wednesday night.
The girl will appear in the pageant opening
preliminary contest dressed in a bathing suit."

Why does a girl dress in a bathing suit
in a contest? Isn't this a terrific and shame-

ful price for popularity and to be crowned queen? There are thousands of eyes of men who want to see that body, too, and judges and crowds appraise it, and so our girls dress in a very skimpy bathing suit. Why, oh, why? Here's another quote: "She has shown the judges how she looks in a bathing suit." Think of it! Latter-day Saint girls, showing judges, showing men, showing the world *how* they look in a bathing suit. Abominable! Now, brothers and sisters, I'm going to read to you a few lines from a brother who feels just as I do, and just as your prophet seemed to feel. He went to see one of the games at a western university, and he wrote:

"It was a demonstration of baton twirling. Immediately the atmosphere changed. The girls in glittering drum majorette costumes marched onto the playing field. The costumes were of the briefest, leaving the girls nude from the hips down, and with tight and form-revealing clothes scantily covering their torsos. In these garbs, patterned after burlesque show costumes, they came onto the field, and there in the glare of the afternoon sun they gyrated and pirouetted in the eyes of the huge crowd of spectators.

"I'm sure that the baton twirling of the girls calls for considerable skill, but I'm at a loss to see any relationship between it and the exhibitionism that went along with it. The wolf whistles, the other exclamations, which rose from the student bleachers on the east side of the stadium where both cheering sections were seated, were not a tribute to artistic skill. I sat in the public bleachers of the west side, and the experience was acutely embarrassing to me. I'm sure that these girls are virtuous, sincere, and wholesome, but I cannot think that they would have been either pleased or flattered by the snickers, the suggestive exclamations and the lewd comments which filled the air around me as they performed their act."

Now, we do not need to ape the world. We must be different when there is a right and wrong. We do not have to do anything we do not want to do. We can create our own styles and costumes. Another quote from Seattle, September 13, 1950: "A scholarly research job at the University of Washington was called off Wednesday, because parents objected to the photographing of their daughters in the nude." Thank God for some good Gentile people in Seattle! "Scholarly research job!" My, to what extent have we gone! How low we go to do scholarly work sometimes!

Now another phase of this. I have just clipped a picture from *The Deseret News*. "This lovely bride of the mid-autumn social season will be Miss .... Stately rites in the Salt Lake Temple will be performed for this prominent couple. Mr .... has recently fulfilled an L.D.S. mission." When you see this picture, you'll know what I'm talking about. It appeared in the newspaper, and why any Latter-day Saint girl or woman would permit her undressed body to be published to a hundred thousand observers, I cannot understand.

Here's another one: Just from last week's paper: "Marriage ceremonies will be solemnized in the Salt Lake Temple, uniting Miss .... and Mr. .... in the Salt Lake Temple." Undressed bodies! Here is another naming the Logan Temple. I've said enough about this, perhaps, but I'm positive, brothers and sisters, that the gowns that we wear can be a tremendous factor in the gradual breakdown of our love of virtue, our steadfastness in chastity. I'm sure of it!

Now, sometimes we get a little careless, and we think it doesn't do very much harm to go into a tavern. Keep away from the taverns. They are hell holes. Don't ever let yourselves be found there a single time, and don't ever take the first drink. You know what happens: one smoke, one glass of beer, and it's step by step to drinking, and drunkenness, and a great many of other problems follow.

I want to read to you another scripture, from the 59th Section of the Doctrine and Covenants. It has one special thought in it that I would like to leave with you. The Lord is reiterating the Ten Commandments here, through the Prophet Joseph Smith:

"Wherefore, I give unto them a commandment, saying thus: Thou shalt love the Lord thy God with all thy heart, with all thy might, mind, and strength; and in the name of Jesus Christ thou shalt serve him.

"Thou shalt love thy neighbor as thyself. Thou shalt not steal; neither commit adultery, nor kill, *nor do anything like unto it.*" (D.&C. 59:5.)

What is there "like unto" fornication or adultery? This "petting" if I may use that term is "like unto it" and is mental adultery. Jesus gave it to us clearly. He said: "Ye have heard that it was said by them of old time, Thou shalt not commit adultery?

"But I say unto you —" this was the new law, the high law — "But I say unto you, That whosoever looketh on a woman to lust after her hath committed adultery with her already in his heart." (Matthew 5:27-38.)

Mental adultery! Physical adultery! Now, you sisters, know this: that your boy friends will not love nor respect you if they have freedom in fondling you. Some of them will test you. If you are strong they will honor you, but if you yield they will not love you for it. Can you not distinguish between love on one hand and lust on the other? Satisfying desires? Don't you know that often he boasts to his fellows how far he could go with you? Do not let him touch you! Give your life in protecting yourself before you let an evil experience of this kind come to you, And, paraphrasing: "Whosoever looketh on a man to lust after him hath committed adultey with him already in her heart." It fits both men and women, and it is sin. It is a grievous sin also for our boys to test and tempt. How low and degenerate is the boy who pursues to the point of denial!

Now, our Latter-day Saint boys and girls are the finest in the world. There is no group anywhere from ocean to ocean that can even compare with them. And yet, there are too many misfortunes. There are too many who have lost themselves. I believe practically every boy and girl grows up with a desire to be righteous. I think youths are fundamentally good. But the devil knows how to destroy them. He knows, young fellows, that he cannot tempt you to murder or to commit adultery immediately, but he knows, too, that if he can get you to sit in your car late enough after the dance or if he can get you to park long enough at the end of the lane, (because he has had thousands of years of experience) he knows that the best boy and the best girl will finally succumb and will fall. He knows that they do have a limit to their resistance.

Most of the professional prostitutes and libertines did not intend to be such. They began generally by having slipped, through temptation, then having fallen and having failed to repent, they lost themselves. Brothers and Sisters, the Lord bless you. This is important. This subject is difficult to talk about. I'd much prefer developing other topics. But when bishops come to me with sad stories of broken homes, frustrated lives, of heartbreak, sorrow, remorse and when I interview people who have had misfortunes, I say to them in near desperation: "What can the Church do to avoid this? What can we do to protect the next generation, the younger ones who are coming along?' Tell me." And invariably this boy or girl will say, "Brother Kimball, it isn't taught frankly enough. We get much sex education, but it damages us. We hear the vulgar all the time. We need warnings frequently — frank warnings from the Church."

Now, before I close, I should say the Lord has given us a great promise. This is a gospel of repentance. It is the gospel of forgiveness; but forgiveness does not come easily. When one has gone down this wide lane to evil, he must come back up the lane, climbing, and it's a hard, hard pull. The way of the transgressor is hard.

"Wherefore teach it unto your children, that all men, everywhere, must repent, or they can in nowise inherit the kingdom of God, for no unclean thing can dwell there or dwell in his presence; for in the language of Adam, Man of Holiness is his name, and the name of his Only Begotten is the Son of Man, even Jesus Christ, a righteous Judge, who shall come in the meridian of time." (Moses 6:57.)

But if a repentant one will fast enough, and pray enough, and weep enough, and serve enough, he can come back, and the gates are still open to him — many of the gates — but he will never be quite what he would have been if there had been no slipping.

Now, brothers and sisters, the Lord bless you to help others. Most of you, I am sure, are clean and sweet and have only one great desire, and that is to keep your virtue, ever to be clean, to give service, and to show gratitude and ever display prayerfulness and worshipfulness. I'm sure of that. But maybe you can help others whom you meet in social groups and in little crowds here and there.

In your own family perhaps your younger brothers and sisters need your sustaining help. When you've saved a soul, you've done the greatest service in all the world.

With your membership in the true church of the Living God you are headed toward salvation and Godhood. The Lord has promised to the valiant "All that I have is thine." To reach those lofty heights and limitless blessings, you must take no chances. Keep your lives sweet and clean and pure, so that there will never be any forfeiture. To do this you will do well to avoid "the very appearance of evil" and "the very approach toward evil." Some of these deadly but unrecognized approaches have been pointed out to you today. "He that hath ears to hear, let him hear." May God help you all to walk steadfastly toward the eternal goals with clean hands and pure hearts, and that your lives may be full and sweet and abundant, I pray, in the name of Jesus Christ, our Redeemer. Amen.

Before It's Too Late

(Excerpt of a Sermon by an unknown Author)

A father, talking to his careless daughter, said:

"I want to speak to you of your mother. It may be that you have noticed a careworn look upon her face lately. Of course, it has not been brought there by any act of yours, still it is your duty to chase it away. I want you to get up tomorrow morning and get breakfast; and when your mother comes, and begins to express her surprise, go right up to her and kiss her on the mouth. You can't imagine how it will brighten her dear face.

"Besides, you owe her a kiss or two. Away back, when you were a little girl, she kissed you when no one else was tempted by your fever-tainted breath and swollen face. You were not as attractive then as you are now. And through those years of childish sunshine and shadows she was always ready to cure, by the magic of a mother's kiss, the dirty, little, chubby hands whenever they were injured in those first skirmishes with the rough old world.

"And then the midnight kiss with which she routed so many sad dreams, so she leaned above your restless pillow, have all been on interest these long, long years.

"Of course, she is not so pretty and kissable as you are.

"Her face has more wrinkles than yours, and yet, if you were sick, that face would appear far more beautiful than an angel's as it hovered over you, watching every opportunity to minister to your comfort, and every one of those wrinkles would seem to be bright wavelets of sunshine chasing each other over the dear face.

"She will leave you one of these days. These burdens, if not lifted from her shoulders, will break her down. Those rough, hard hands that have done so many necessary things for you will be crossed upon her lifeless breast.

"Those neglected lips that gave you your first baby kiss, will be forever closed, and those sad, tired eyes will have opened in eternity and then you will appreciate your mother. Remember her before it's too late."

Be Ye Clean

(Address to the Brigham Young University Studentbody
at Provo, Utah on May 4, 1954 by Elder Spencer W.
Kimball of the Council of the Twelve)

This is a true story. The characters are real.

It was a long-distance call; that was quite apparent, for as I picked up the receiver I could hear the coins dropping in a far away coin box, then a voice asked, "Brother Kimball?"

I answered, "Yes."

It was a young man's voice saying, "I have a very personal problem. Could I bring my girl friend and come to see you?"

"Of course," I said, and a time was arranged.

It was not long until the young couple was announced. The deep pleasant voice was just what one might expect from the tall, athletic youth who possessed it. He was well proportioned, and like King David, "ruddy and withal of a beautiful countenance and goodly to look to." (I Samuel 16:12)

With him was a lovely girl, slight of frame and beautiful of face and form. They were both dressed well, and it was evident that they were from cultured homes. It was also obvious that they loved each other, for as they sat together across the desk from me he reached quietly for her hand.

The melodious voice was hesitant and a bit choked with emotions as he introduced his girl friend, and there was pleading in their eyes. "We are in difficulty, Brother Kimball," he said, "we have broken the law of chastity. We have defiled ourselves. We prayed and fasted and agonized and finally came to the conclusion that we must try to make adjustments."

I asked them a few questions. It was evident they had been treading deep waters. The girl took over the conversation, "I had convinced myself that I was able to take care of myself, that I would never commit this abhorrent sin. I have heard the brethren say repeatedly that necking and petting were sins in their own right, but I would not let myself believe it."

I let them tell the story without interruption, feeling it would enable them to unload the heavy burden they were carrying.

The boy was now speaking. He was self-accusing. "That Junior Prom date was a very special one," he continued. "But it turned out to be a tragic one, the beginning of sorrows. When I saw my sweetheart coming downstairs that night, I thought no girl was ever so beautiful and so sweet. We danced through the evening; and then when we sat in the car, long and silently afterward, my thoughts became unruly as we made love. Neither of us dreamed of what was happening to us," he said, "but all the elements were there to break down resistance. We did not notice time — the hours passed. Our usual elementary necking gradually developed into petting. There were other nights — the bars were down. We loved each other so much that we convinced ourselves that it was not so wrong since we sort of belonged to each other anyway. Where we ended the other night became the starting point this night, and we continued on and on, and finally it happened — the terrible thing happened. We had vowed it would never envelope us. And then when it was late — so late — so everlastingly late, we awoke to our plight. We hated ourselves. We mentally thrashed ourselves. She suggested we pray, but I told her I felt too unworthy. I wanted to hide from the Lord, from everybody. Oh, Brother Kimball, what can we do? Is it unpardonable? Are we lost forever? Can we ever gain forgiveness?"

His voice broke and there was a heavy silence.

I sat deep in thought, praying fervently that the Lord would inspire me to assist them.

They seemed to want to talk. It was as though a great flood of feelings needed release.

"I am so ashamed," she said. "I was not guiltless. When we reached home, he turned off the engine. We became quiet; the conversation lagged; and the thing began to happen against which we had been warned and rewarned. The goodnight kiss was a warm, passionate, long-sustained one, and we lingered longer. When I knelt at my bed that night I asked the Lord to forgive me, and I think (at that moment) I honestly intended never to repeat the process."

"I felt I loved him as no girl ever loved one before. He was good, but he was human. The necking evolved into petting sooner each night, and a new pattern was being established. I felt guilty when I went in. I didn't feel much like praying. Why should I? What use to pray when I would likely continue. I wasn't so sure I wanted to quit. It wasn't so bad anyway, was it? We hadn't committed fornication and wouldn't — certainly we wouldn't. That we knew."

"Little did we realize that each time there were new excesses. And suddenly we awakened to the fact that we had lost our virtue totally — had lost that most priceless thing — we had committed that most abominable sin. I loathed myself. Why had I not listened? Why had I disregarded counsel? Why had I not run, screamed, fought, died? There was no sleep for me this night. I was unclean. I bathed, scrubbed, washed my hair, put on fresh clothes. I was still filthy. I remembered the lepers in Bible days — how they stood afar off and cried to an approaching person, 'unclean, unclean.' I felt like a leper, like hiding, like avoiding everyone. My soul cried out in agony. Could I keep others from hearing the sobbing of my heart?"

"In the sleepless nights were horrible dreams, nightmares. Why must I be so plagued? Other young people had done this terrible thing. It did not seem to wreck them. They seemed to pass it off with a shrug of the shoulders, but I —

"Hell? Yes, this is hell. We always thought of hell as far-away, mythical and abstract thing, but we've found it — we've tasted it — it is bitter, very bitter. Why weren't youth warned of these horrors? Then I remembered we had been warned, all our lives. Why had we not listened? Why did we remain in the car late at night after we should have said goodnight?"

She could not stop. It was like the flood of the waters escaping from a broken reservoir. "A thousand thoughts ran through my mind," she said, "ugly accusing thoughts — when I ate, when I walked, when I prayed. The ghost memory taunted me."

And now they sat very still, very close, waiting, almost breathlessly. "Children of disobedience," I thought. My heart was sobbing for them; "Please, Father, bles me that I may help them."

"Can we ever be fogiven, Brother Kimball," they asked plaintively.

"Yes, beloved youth," I replied, "the Lord and His Church can forgive, but not easily. 'The way of the transgressor is hard.' It ever has been — it always will be. The Lord Himself said:

> I tell thee thou shalt not depart thence till thou hast paid the very last mite. (Luke 12:59)

But, in His goodness, He provided for us a way to forgiveness. One may do as he pleases, but he cannot evade responsibility. He may break laws, but he cannot avoid penalties. One gets by with nothing. No one ever gets anything for nothing. God is just.

> Be not deecived, said Paul, God is not mocked, for whatsoever a man soweth, that shall he also reap. (Galatians 6:7)

Again:

> Mortify therefore your members which
> are upon the earth; fornication, unclean-
> liness, inordinate affection, evil concu-
> piscence and covetousness, . . . for which
> things' sake, the wrath of God cometh
> on the children of disobedience. (Collos-
> sians 3:5-6)

Serious as are these abominable things,
there is forgiveness conditioned upon total
repentance. The Prophet Amulek quoted the
Lord:

> . . . and he hath said that no unclean
> thing can inherit the kingdom of heav-
> en; therefore, how can ye be saved
> except ye inherit the kingdom of heav-
> en? Therefore, ye cannot be saved in
> your sins. (Alma 11:37)

And Isaiah:

> . . . Let the wicked forsake his way
> . . . and let him return unto the Lord,
> . . . for He will abundantly pardon.
> (Isaiah 55:6-7)

Yes, the Lord will forgive. How *grateful*
we all must be for this saving principle!

> Behold, he who has repented his sins,
> the same is forgiven, and I the Lord
> remember them no more. (Doctrine &
> Covenants 58:42)

How *glorious* this promise!

> . . . though your sins be as scarlet,
> they shall be as white as snow; though
> they be red like crimson, they shall be
> as wool. (Isaiah 1:18)

The young couple seemed to relax a bit.
Hope was returning. "That is certainly com-
forting," said the young man, "but how may
we obtain this forgiveness which we so much
desire?"

I explained: One must come to a realization of the seriousness of the error. There are
sins which cannot be forgiven, but fortunate-
ly most can be remitted. They range from the
simple improprieties and indiscretions to the
shedding of innocent blood and denying the
Holy Ghost, both of which are unpardonable.
Neither of you has committed the sin against
the Holy Ghost for that requires more knowledge than either of you has. Neither of you
has committed murder, and therefore we may

say that every error that you may have committed is in the forgivable category. Since Cain killed his brother Abel, there have been in the world all these accumulating vices. There are sins which are known to others and those which are secretly hidden. Every one is against ourselves and God, for they limit our progress, curtail our development and estrange us from good people, good influences and from our Lord. The early apostles and prophets mention sins which seemed completely reprehensible to them. Some of them were adultery, being without natural affection, lustfulness, infidelity, incontinence, filthy communications, impurity, inordinate affection, inventors of evil things. Today we call them necking, petting, fornication, sex perversion, masturbation. Included are every hidden and secret sin, and all unholy and impure thoughts and practices.

Next to the unpardonable sins come the diabolical crimes of sexual impurity which raise their ugly heads in many different forms, including aberrations of self-pollution and the abhorrent and unnatural practices involving other people. Conscience tells the individual when he is entering forbidden worlds and continues to prick until silenced by the will or by sin's constant pressures. Can anyone truthfully say he did not know such things were wrong? These unholy practices, whatever may be their unmentionable names with all their approaches and numerous manifestations, are condemned by the Lord and His Church. Some may be more heinous than others, but all are sin, in spite of the statements to the contrary of those who falsely pretend to know. The Lord's prophets declare they are not normal. The world may have its norm; the Church has a different one. It may be considered normal by the people of the world to use tobacco; the Church's norm is a high plane where smoking is not done. The world's norm may permit men and women social drinking and cocktail parties; the Lord's Church lifts its people to a norm of total abstinence. The world may countenance pre-marital sex experiences, but the Lord and His Church condemn in no uncertain terms any and every sex relationship outside of marriage, and even indecent and uncontrolled ones within marriage. And so, though many self-styled

authorities justify these practices as a normal
release, the Church condemns them and could
not knowingly send such people, *unrepentant*
into the mission field or give them places
of trust or position of responsibility. Such
unholy practices were condemned by ancient
prophets and are today condemned by the
Church.

Paul lashed out against the unholy evidences of the vulgar mind and of uncontrolled
passion and desire:

> Wherefore God also gave them up to
> uncleanness through the lust of their
> own hearts, to dishonor their own bodies
> between themselves . . . (Romans 1:24)

There are those who with vicious tendencies or weak wills say: "The Lord made me
this way, gave me these desires and passions,
and He will not condemn me." This is untrue.
James said:

> Let no man say when he is tempted,
> I am tempted of God, for God cannot be
> tempted with evil, neither tempeth He
> any man. (James 1:13)

Let him who has evil tendencies be honest and acknowledge his weakness. I tell you the Lord places no sin in our lives. He has made no man wicked. We are sons and daughters of God, possessing seeds of godhood. We are not limited by instinct as are the beasts. We have godly power to grow and to overcome and become perfect. Sin was permitted in the world and Satan permitted to tempt us, but we have our free agency. We may sin or live righteously, but we cannot escape responsibility. To blame our sin upon the Lord, saying it is inherent and cannot be controlled, is cheap and cowardly. To blame our sins upon our parents and our upbringing is the way of the escapist. One's parents may have failed; his backgrounds may have been frustrating, but as sons and daughters of a living God we have within ourselves the power to rise above our circumstances, to change our lives. Man *can* change human nature. Man *must* transform his life. We will be punished for our sins. We *must* accept responsibility for our sins. We *can* overcome. We *must* control and master self.

The lovely girl now said: "While we knew our intimacies were indiscreet, we did not fully realize the implications."

"I am sure of that," I said, "that is why
I elaborate on them. Since courtship is pre-
lude to marriage and encourages close asso-
ciations, many have convinced themselves
that intimacies are legitimate — a part of the
courting process. Many have cast off bridle
and harness and relaxed restraints. Instead
of remaining in the field of simple expressions
of affection, some have turned themselves
loose to fondling, commonly called "necking"
with its intimate contacts and its passionate
kissing. It is an insidious practice leading
to other vices. Necking is a younger member
of this unholy family. Its bigger sister is
called 'petting.' When the intimacies have
reached this stage they are surely the sins
condemned by the Savior:

> Ye have heard that it was said by them
> of old time, Thou shalt not commit
> adultery, but I say unto you, that who-
> soever looketh on a woman to lust after
> her hath committed adultery with her
> already in his heart. (Matthew 5:27-28)

Who would say that he or she who pets
has not become lustful, has not become passionate? Who would say that there has not

been mental and physical adultery? Is it not this most abominable practice against which God rebuked in His modern reiteration of the Ten Commandments:

> Thou shalt not steal; neither commit adultery, nor kill, nor do anything like unto it.

What, may I ask you, is like unto adultery if it is not petting? Did not the Lord recognize that this heinous sin is but the devil's softening process for the final acts of adultery? Can any person in the light of the Lord's scriptures pursue the path of petting with clear conscience? Can anyone convince himself that this is not deep sin?

The youthful pair now had many questions which carried me on in explanation. "Are fornication and adultery the same?" they asked.

An older sister in this unholy family, most destructive in her diabolical effects and requiring severe punishment is sexual impurity called fornication when committed by the unmarried and adultery when committed by those who are wed. The two terms are often interchanged in scripture. Another vicious

sister, hiding behind expediency, is the ugly
one of illegal abortion. One crime seems to
demand another, and sometimes cowardly
adulterous folks, because of possible scandal
and social ostracism and who have not the
courage to meet and solve problems, add to
their sexual sin that sin of destroying a child.
These twin crimes rate very high in the
category of horrible ones.

When we say that the sexual sins are forgivable, this does not mean they are easily
overcome. Paul said:

> . . . no whoremonger, nor unclean per-
> son, . . . hath any inheritance in the
> kingdom of Christ and of God. Let no
> man deceive you with vain words; for
> because of these things cometh the
> wrath of God upon the children of dis-
> obedience. Be not ye therefore partakers
> with them. (Ephesians 5:5-7)

And Nephi writes:

> . . . the Kingdom of God is not filthy,
> and there canont any unclean thing en-
> ter into the kingdom of God; wherefore
> there must needs be a place of filthi-

> ness prepared for that which is filthy
> . . . (I Nephi 15:34)

The Lord commands:

> Thou shalt not commit adultery . . .
> and he that committeth adultery and
> repenteth not, shall be cast out. (Doc-
> trine and Covenants 42:24)

The young man was agitated now and asked: "Does 'cast out' mean excommunication? And must we suffer that penalty?"

And I answered:

The Lord has indicated that 'the plaster must be the size of the sore'; if one has offended many, he must be chastized before many, and if the offense is known to few, then the adjustment involves few. Every *unrepentent* transgressor should be handled, and if he continues rebellious should be disfellowshipped or excommunicated. One disfellowshipped is usually forbidden to exercise his priesthood and is denied the blessings of the Church such as Sacrament, temple privileges and Church activity. Excommunication is a complete severing of all ties. One loses membership, the Holy Ghost, priesthood, sealings, and all Church privileges. If the transgression is known and is a public scandal, the individual is sometimes permitted to make a public adjustment 'not to the members but to the elders' so that all who have heard of the sin may also know of the repentence. This is a clearing privilege which everyone involved in a publicly known scandal should grasp gladly.

The young woman asked: "Then repentance and publicity are controlling factors?"

"Yes, my sister, a transgressor whose sin is secret and has been voluntarily confessed and whose repentance is without reservations can be forgiven in secret by proper authorities. Even the Lord could not forgive one without sincere repentance.

> . . . He hath said that no unclean thing can inherit the kingdom of heaven; . . . Therefore, ye cannot be saved in your sins. (Alma 11:37)

And being transgressors:

> . . . we would fain be glad if we could command the rocks and the mountains to

> fall upon us to hide us from his pres-
> ence. (Alma 12:14)

"That is just the way I feel now," the boy whispered.

Christ postulated:

> And no unclean thing can enter into
> his Kingdom; therefore nothing entereth
> into his rest save it be those who have
> washed their garments in my blood . . .
> (3 Nephi 27:19)

The young folks were listening intently but with growing apprehension, and she finally asked: "How then can we, being so un-clean, ever get into the kingdom of Heaven?"

I answered: It is true — no unclean thing can enter the Kingdom. but a totally repentant thing is no longer an unclean thing; a fully purged and forgiven adulterer is no longer an adulterer. He who has "washed his garments" is presumed to be free from filth.

This splendid young couple had made their decision. They were ready to comply with any requirements no matter how severe. They drew a little closer to each other and

asked: "Brother Kimball, what must we do?"
I continued:

Repentance seems to fall into five steps:

1. Sorrow for sin.

2. Abandonment of sin.

3. Confession of sin.

4. Restitution for sin.

5. Doing the will of the Lord.

1. SORROW FOR SIN

To be sorry for our sin we must know something of its serious implications. When fully convicted, we condition our minds to follow such processes as will rid us of the effects of the sin. We are sorry. We are willing to make amends, pay penalties, to suffer even to excommunication if necessary. Paul wrote:

> For Godly sorrow worketh repentance
> to salvation not to be repented of, but
> the sorrow of the world worketh death.
> (2 Corinthians 7:9-10)

If one is sorry only because his sin was uncovered, his repentance is not complete. Godly sorrow which causes one to harness desire and to determine to do right regardless of consequences — this kind of sorrow brings righteousness and will work toward forgiveness.

2. ABANDONMENT OF SIN

It is best when one discontinues his error because of his realization of the gravity of his sin and when he is willing to comply with the laws of God. The thief may abandon his evil in prison, but true repentance would have him forsake it before his arrest and return his booty without enforcement. The sex offender who voluntarily ceases his unholy practices is headed toward forgiveness. Alma said:

> Blessed are they who humble themselves without being compelled to be humble . . . (Alma 32:16)

And the Lord:

> By this ye may know if a man repenteth of his sins — behold he will . . . forsake them. (Doctrine and Covenants 58:43)

The discontinuance must be a permanent one. True repentance does not permit repetition. Peter said:

> For if after they have escaped the pollu-
> tions of the world . . . they are again en-
> tangled therein . . . it had been better
> for them not to have known the way of
> righteousness than, after they have
> known it, to turn from the holy com-
> mandment . . . (like) The dog is turned
> to his own vomit again, and the sow
> that was washed to her wallowing in
> the mire. (2 Peter 2:20-22)

Forgiveness is not assured if one reverts to
early sins. The Lord said:

> . . . go your ways and sin no more; but
> unto that soul who sinneth shall the
> former sins return . . . (Doctrine and
> Covenants 82:7)

The Savior said to the adulteress taken in
the act of sin: "Go thy way and sin no more."
And Paul:

> Let him that stole, steal no more . . .
> (Ephesians 4:28)

3. CONFESSION OF SIN

The confession of sin is an important ele-
ment in repentance. Many offenders have

seemed to feel that a few prayers to the Lord were sufficient. They have thus justified themselves in hiding their sins.

> He that covereth his sins shall not prosper, but whoso confesseth and forsaketh them shall have mercy . . . (Proverbs 28:13)

> By this ye may know if a man repenteth of his sins — behold he will confess them and forsake them. (Doctrine and Covenants 58:43)

Especially grave errors such as sexual sins shall be confessed to the bishop as well as to the Lord. There are two remissions which one might wish to have. First, the forgiveness from the Lord, and second, the forgiveness of the Lord's Church through its leaders. As soon as one has an inner conviction of his sins, he should go to the Lord in 'mighty prayer' as did Enos and never cease his supplications until he shall, like Enos, receive the assurance that his sins have been forgiven by the Lord. It is unthinkable that God absolves serious sins upon a few requests. He is likely to wait until there has been long sustained repentance as evidenced by a willingness to comply with all His other requirements. No priest nor elder is authorized to this act for the Church. The Lord has a consistent, orderly plan. Every soul in stakes is given a bishop who, by the very nature of his calling and ordination, is a 'judge in Israel.' The bishop is one's best earthly friend. He will hear the problems, judge the seriousness thereof, determine the degree of repentance and decide if it warrants an eventual forgiveness. He does this as the earthly representative of God, the master physician, the master psychologist, the master psychiatrist. If repentance is sufficient he may waive penalties which is tantamount to forgiveness. The bishop claims no authority to absolve sins, but he does share the burden, waive penalties, relieve tension and strain and he may assure a continuation of activity. He will keep the whole matter most confidential.

Some missionaries have foolishly carried with them their secret, unadjusted guilt into the field and suffered seriously in the effort to get and retain the spirit of the mission. The conflict in the soul was most frustrating. But he who totally repented, voluntarily con-

fessed and cleared his difficulty so far as
possible, triumphed in his work and enjoyed
sweet peace.

We read:

> . . . for I, the Lord, forgive sins, and
> am merciful unto those who confess
> their sins with humble hearts . . . (Doc-
> trine and Covenants 61:2)

The Lord says:

> By this ye may know that a man repent-
> eth of his sins, behold he will confess
> them and forsake them. (Doctrine and
> Covenants 58:43)

And Paul:

> For with the heart man believeth unto
> righteousness; and with the mouth con-
> fession is made unto salvation. (Romans
> 10:10)

In the days of the Nephites the Church leaders received confessions and forgave or excommunicated accordingly.

4. RESTITUTION FOR SIN

When one is humble in sorrow, has uncon-
ditionally abandoned the evil, confessed to

those assigned by the Lord, he should next restore insofar as possible that which was damaged. If he burglarized, he should return to the rightful owner that which was stolen. Perhaps one reason murder is unforgivable is that having taken a life, the murderer cannot restore it. Restitution in full is not possible. Also having robbed one of virtue, it is impossible to give it back.

However, the truly repentant soul will usually find things which can be done to restore to some extent. The true spirit of repentance demands this. Ezekiel taught:

> . . . if the wicked give again that he has robbed, walk in the statutes of life, without committing iniquity; he shall surely live. (Ezekiel 33:14-15)

Moses taught:

> If a man shall steal an ox or a sheep, . . . he shall restore five oxen for an ox, and four sheep for a sheep . . . (Exodus 22:1)

A pleading sinner must also forgive all people of all offenses committed against himself. The Lord is under no obligation to for-

give us unless our hearts are fully purged
of all hate, bitterness and accusations against
all others.

5. DO THE WILL OF THE FATHER

The Lord in His preface to modern revela-
tions gave us the fifth and one of the most
difficult requirements to forgiveness. He says:

> I, the Lord cannot look upon sin with
> the least degree of allowance. Neverthe-
> less, he that repents and *does the com-
> mandments of the Lord* shall be for-

given. (Doctrine and Covenants 1:31-32)
Under the humiliation of a guilty conscience,
with the possibility of detection and conse-
quent scandal and shame, with a striving
spirit urging toward adjustment, the first
steps of sorrow, abandonment, confession and
restitution must now be followed by the never-
ending requirement of doing the commandments. Obviously this can hardly be done in
a day, a week, a month or a year. This is an
effort extending through the balance of life.
"Unto the End," is an often used phrase in
the scriptures:

> If thou wilt do good, yea, and hold out
> faithful to the end, thou shalt be saved
> in the kingdom of God . . . (Doctrine
> and Covenants 6:13)

> . . . he only is saved who endureth unto
> the end. Even so Amen. (Doctrine and
> Covenants 53:7)

Good works are the evidences of fruits of
repentance. The Redeemer expresses this
thought:

> Ye shall know them by their fruits. Do
> men gather grapes of thorns, or figs of
> thistles?

> A good tree cannot bring forth evil
> fruit; neither can a corrupt tree bring
> forth good fruit . . .

> Wherefore by their fruits shall ye know
> them. (Matthew 7:16-20)

The Lord said:

> But he that has committed adultery and
> repents with all his heart and forsaketh
> it and doeth it no more, thou shalt
> forgive. (Doctrine and Covenants 42:25)

Now the phrase "with all his heart" is vital. There can be no reservations. It must be an all-out unconditional surrender. The mere abandonment of the specific sin, and even the confession of it are not sufficient to save. If the transgressor neglects his tithing, misses his meetings, breaks the Sabbath or fails in his family prayers and other responsibilities, he is not wholly repentant. The Lord knows, as does the individual, the degree of contrition, and the reward will be according to deserts, for God is just. Feigning repentance or bluffing is futile, for both the transgressor and the Lord can evaluate and recognize insincerity and hypocrisy. One may fool his fellowmen sometimes, but himself and his Lord never. Yet the devout, repenting soul has claim upon the mercy of the Lord.

Doing the commandments includes many activities. General good works and constructive attitudes are supplemented by the bearing of testimony and the saving of souls. The Lord says:

> For I will forgive you of your sins with this commandment . . . remain steadfast in your minds in solemnity and the spirit

of prayer, in bearing testimony to all the world . . . (Doctrine and Covenants 84:61)

Nevertheless, ye are blessed, for the testimony which ye have borne is recorded in heaven for the angels to look upon; . . . and your sins are forgiven you. (Doctrine and Covenants 62:3)

And James indicated that each good deed, each testimony, each proselyting effort, each safeguard thrown about others is like a blanket over ones own sins, or like a deposit against an overdraft in the bank.

Brethren, if any of you do err from the truth, and one convert him; . . . he which converteth the sinner from the error of his way shall save a soul from death, and shall hide a multitude of sins. (James 5:19-20)

And unto him that repenteth and sanctifieth himself before the Lord shall be given eternal life. (Doctrine and Covenants 133:62)

Not everyone that saith unto me Lord, Lord, shall enter into the kingdom of heaven, but he that doeth the will of my Father which is in heaven. (Matthew 7:21)

I commend to you the book of Enos which records in inspiring detail how a transgressor after long strugglings and continuous crying mightily unto the Lord through the long hours of the day and then extending into the night, finally obtained forgiveness from the Lord.

* * *

And so my beloved young couple, as you leave my office, remember to obtain forgiveness from the Lord and His Church and retain for yourselves the blessings — the one must be convicted of sin, bow the knee in monumental humility, forsake the sin and fortify himself against repetition. He must confess the error to his bishop or other Church authority, cleansing and purging himself of all that was vile. He must take restitution by restoring so far as possible that which was damaged and must forgive all who have given him offense, and finally he must live all of the commandments of the Lord, bringing forth fruits meet for repentance. And when he has fasted enough, wept enough, prayed enough and suffered enough and when his heart is right, he may expect that forgiveness will come and with it that glorious peace which passeth understanding.

We knelt and each prayed fervently. The young couple — mellowed, repentant and determined, thanked me and departed hand in hand.

God bless you all my young brothers and sisters that you may see with your eyes and hear with your ears and understand with your hearts and protect yourselves from the sins of the world. This I pray in the name of Jesus Christ, Amen.

Except Ye Repent

(Excerpts from an address titled "Except Ye Repent"
by Spencer W. Kimball, given at the Sunday morning
session of the 120th Semi-Annual General Conference,
October 2, 1949, in the Salt Lake Tabernacle. (Address
printed in the Improvement Era issue reporting on
this conference)

. . . I find in this Church many people
who amaze me with their close approach
toward perfection, but I do find as I go about
the Church, some who need this principle
of repentance. I thank the Lord for this
glorious principle. I find parents who have
lost the natural affection for their children.
I find children who disown and disclaim their
parents and evade responsibility concerning
them. I find, sometimes, husbands who desert
their wives and their children, and who use
almost every pretext to justify such action.
I find wives who are demanding, unworthy,
quarrelsome, and who are unco-operative and
selfish and worldly, provoking such action.
I find those who gossip and bear false witness against their neighbors. I find brethren
who hale each other into the courts on trivial
matters that could have been settled by themselves. I find blood brothers and sisters, who

fight over inheritances and bring each other into the courts of the land and drag before the public the most intimate and personal family secrets, bringing all of the skeletons out of the closets, leaving nothing sacred, little regard for one another, interested only in that which they might acquire by such action. I saw one family split wide apart, half of the brothers and sisters on one side, and half on the other, in a most disgraceful feud. At the funeral half of them sat on one side of the aisle and half on the other. They would not speak to each other. The property involved was worth only a few thousand dollars, and yet they are avowed enemies. I have seen people in wards and branches who impugn the motives of the authorities and of each other and make them "offender for a word." I have seen people in branches where they have broken wide apart and say unkind things about each other and will hardly speak to one another. They bring into their meetings the spirit of the evil one, instead of the spirit of Christ.

I have seen husbands and wives, living under the same roof, who are selfish, unbend-

ing and unforgiving, who with their misunder-
standings have hardened their hearts and
poisoned their minds. Then I have seen many
people who have become offended at Church
authorities, their ward, stake, mission, aux-
iliary and priesthood leaders, for things which
have been said, or were imagined to have
been said or thought.

To the children who are unkind to their
parents the Lord has said, "Ye hypocrites,"
(Matt. 15:7), "He that curseth father and
mother, let him die the death." (*Ibid.*, 15:5.)
To the intolerant God has said: "What God
hath cleansed, that call not thou common."
(Acts 11:9.) To the gossip he has said from
Sinai: "Thou shalt not bear false witness.
. . ." (Ex. 20:16.) To those who would impugn motives he said: "Judge not, that ye
be not judged." (Matt. 7:1.) And to those
who would criticize the authorities and use
them as stumbling blocks, who would ab-
sent themselves from their meetings, who
would fail to pay their tithes and other ob-
ligations because of fancied offenses, I would
like to read from the Doctrine and Covenants,
"Cursed are all those that shall lift up the

heel against mine anointed, saith the Lord, and cry they have sinned when they have not sinned before me, saith the Lord, but have done that which was meet in mine eyes, and which I commanded them.

"But those who cry transgression do it because they are the servants of sin, and are the children of disobedience themselves.

"And those who swear falsely against my servants . . .

Their basket shall not be full, their houses and their barns shall perish, and they themselves shall be despised by those that flattered them.

"They shall not have right to the priesthood, nor their posterity after them from generation to generation." (Sec. 121:16-18, 20-21.) And to all who sin in devious ways, the Savior says: ". . . except ye repent, ye shall all likewise perish." (Luke 13:5.)

* * *

As I read the scriptures I find that all the various sins are condemned. May I name only a few whom he calls to repentance:

the murderer and the adulterer and the thief,
the proud, the coveter, the drinker, the
smoker, the ungrateful, the liar, the gambler,
the drunkard, the selfish, the unforgiving,
the accuser, the defrauder, the gossip, the
profane, the vulgar, the intolerant, the mali-
cious, the idler, the persecutor, the envious,
and the jealous, and to all these the Lord
says: "Repent and walk more uprightly before me." (D & C 5:21.)

* * *

Now, in Proverbs 28:13, the Lord inspired his prophet to say, "He that covereth
his sins shall not prosper: but whoso con-
fesseth and forsaketh them shall have mercy."

* * *

To obtain forgiveness of our sins, we must
forgive.

"My disciples, in days of old, sought occasion against one another and forgave not
one another in their hearts; and for this
evil they were afflicted and sorely chastened.

"Wherefore, I say unto you, that ye ought
to forgive one another; for he that forgiveth

not his brother his trespasses standeth condemned before the Lord; for there remaineth in him the greater sin." (D & C 64:8-9.)

* * *

An impressive example of unholy judging comes to us in the Lord's parable of the unmerciful servant who owed to his lord ten thousand talents but being unable to pay, his lord "commanded him to be sold, and his wife, and children and all that he had, and payment to be made." The servant fell down and begged for a moratorium, and when the compassionate lord had loosed him and forgiven his debt this conscienceless person straightway found one of his fellowservants who owed him an hundred pence and taking him by the throat demanded payment in full and upon failure of the debtor cast him into prison. When the lord heard of this rank injustice he chastised the unmerciful servant: "O thou wicked servant, I forgave thee all that debt, because thou desiredst me.

"Shouldest not thou also have had compassion on thy fellowservant, even as I had pity on thee?

"And his lord was wroth, and delivered him to the tormentors, till he should pay all that was due unto him." (Matt. 18:24-34.) Then the Redeemer summarizing said to his disciples: "So likewise shall my heavenly Father do also unto you, if ye from your hearts forgive not every one his brother their trespasses." (*Ibid.*, 18:35.) According to my Bible the Roman penny is an eight of an ounce of silver, while the talent is 750 ounces. Accordingly the unmerciful servant was forgiven 600,000 units but would not forgive one unit.

* * *

I met a woman once, demanding and critical. She accused her stake president of harshness and would have displaced him if she could. She had committed adultery, and yet with her comparative debt of 600,000 pence she had the temerity to criticize her leader with a hundred pence debt. I also knew a young man who complained at his bishop and took offense at the leader's inefficiency and his grammatical errors, yet he himself had in his life sins comparable to the talents, and

had the effrontery to accuse his bishop with
weaknesses comparable only to the pence.

* * *

Remember, that we must forgive even if
our offender did not repent and ask forgiveness. Stephen yet in his young life had mas-
tered this principle. His accusers, unable to
find anything against him other than fancied
blasphemy, stoned him to death. Not waiting
for them to repent, Stephen displayed his
saintliness by using his last breath to forgive
them saying: "Lord, lay not this sin to their
charge." (Acts 7:60.)

* * *

It frequently happens that offenses are
committed when the offender is not aware
of it. Something he has said or done is
misconstrued or misunderstood. The offended
one treasures in his heart the offense, adding
to it such other things as might give fuel
to the fire and justify his conclusions. Perhaps this is one of the reasons why the Lord
requires that the offended one should make
the overtures toward peace. He says: "And

if thy brother or sister offended thee, thou shalt take him or her and thee alone; and if he or she confess thou shalt be reconciled." (D & C 43:88.)

And this reconciliation suggests also forgetting. Unless you forget, have you forgiven? A woman in a branch in the mission field where there had been friction finally capitulated and said, "Yes. I will forgive the others, but I have an eternal memory." Certainly she had not fulfilled the law of forgiving. She was meeting the letter, but not the spirit of it. Frequently we say we forgive, then permit the grievance to continue to poison and embitter us.

The Lord forgets when he has forgiven, and certainly must we. He inspired Isaiah to say: "I, even I, am he that blotteth out thy transgressions for mine own sake, and will not remember thy sins." (Isaiah 43:25.)

Unfinished Business

(Excerpt of an address to the Brigham Young
University studentbody by Elder Harold B. Lee,
January, 1954)

The story opens with a young woman on
the train, alone with her thoughts, on her
way to visit her dying father. For the hun-
dredth time she opened her purse, took out
the telegram that read simply. "Father criti-
cally ill. Come at once, Mother." All through
the journey the daughter prayed that the
Lord would keep him alive until she could
arrive and see him again. Then somewhat
guiltily she had to say to herself, "Well, over
the years we have taken Father more or
less just as a matter of course." He was a
necessity; he provided for their food, clothes,
and shelter, but now to realize that he was
in imminent danger of slipping away, being
taken by death, caused a desire that she could
be close to him again, that she could roll
back the years and see him again as she
had seen him in her childhood days. Father
was in a coma when she arrived, but a few
hours later he slipped quietly away. She was
assigned by the family to the task of going

through his personal papers and taking care of what the family called the "unfiinshed business."

She went carefully to her task to make sure that there was nothing that he wished to have done that would be left undone. As she searched in a inside pocket of his coat, she came upon a crumpled bit of paper which showed the effects of having been removed and read, and folded and unfolded many times. This crumpled piece of paper' was a message from a young girl whom her father had befriended, and this letter was a letter of appreciation to this great, noble father. Although this other little girl was not his daughter, he had seemingly clung to the message which this letter conveyed as something of a satisfaction that he hadn't received from his own. The little girl had poured out her heart in gratitude that he had come at a crisis in her life, and she openly expressed her love for his thoughtfulness and kindness to her and his consideration. The daughter laid down the paper and wept because she realized that his own daughter had failed to give her father what this other girl had given and the thing for which he had longed so much. "Unfinished business", but unfortunately the kind of business that she was not permitted to finish! How she wished that she could have rolled back the clock and had a chance to live over some of the years, to have made the life of her father more happy and more joyous than she had done.

Do you have any unfinished business that you would like to take care of while it's yet day?